Statistical analysis in Excel and Python

Copyrighted material

Statistical analysis in Excel and Python is an imprint of Dr Brain Stats ltd.

4 Bronrhiw Avenue Caerphilly CF83 1HF

www.drbrainstats.com

Copyright © 2020 by Dr Brain Stats Limited. All right reserved. No part of this book may be reproduced or transmitted in any form or by means, electronic or mechanical, including photocopying, recording, or by any information storage or retrieval system without prior written permission from the publisher.

Notice of liability

Every effort has been made to ensure that this book contains accurate and current information. However, Dr Brain Stats Ltd and the author shall not be liable for any loss or damage suffered by readers as a result of any information contained herein.

Trademarks

Microsoft ® Windows ® and Excel ® are registered trademarks of Microsoft Corporation. All other trademarks are acknowledged as belonging to their respective companies.

Contents

Introduction 7

1. Introduction to statistics 8

   1.1 What is statistics? 8

   1.2 Mean, median and mode 9

      1.2.1 Example of mean, mode and median 9

   1.3 Measurements 12

      1.3.1 Exercise 1.1: measurements 13

      1.3.2 Solution to exercise 1.1 14

   1.4 Correlation 14

      1.4.1 Example of correlation 15

      1.4.2 Exercise 1.2: correlation 22

      1.4.3 Solution to exercise 1.2 23

   1.5 Simple linear regression 23

      1.5.1 Example of simple linear regression 24

      1.5.2 Exercise 1.3: simple linear regression 29

      1.5.3 Solution to exercise 1.3 30

   1.6 Summary 30

2. Further statistical exploration 31

   2.1 Distribution 31

   2.2 Null hypothesis 32

   2.3 T-tests 33

      2.3.1 Example of t-test 34

      2.3.2 Exercise 2.1: t-tests 36

      2.3.3 Solution to exercise 2.1 37

   2.4 Chi-square 37

      2.4.1 Example of chi-square 38

      2.4.2 Exercise 2.2 chi-square 39

    2.4.3 Solution to exercise 2.2 40

  2.5 Chi-square test of association 40

    2.5.1 Example of chi-square test of association 40

  2.6 Summary 42

3.   Data mining in Excel 43

  3.1 Decisions trees 43

    3.1.1 Definitions 43

    3.1.2 How do we decide the node? 44

  3.2 Converting a continuous variable into a categorical variable 45

    3.2.1 Exercise 3.1 45

    3.2.2 Method1 of creating bins - copy and paste 47

    3.2.3 Method 2 of creating bins - If function 48

  3.3 Decision tree creation 54

    3.3.1 Pivot table 54

    3.3.2 Designing a decision tree in Excel 68

  3.7 Summary 70

4 Introduction to Python 71

  4.1 Spyder 71

  4.2 Excel to Python 73

    4.2.1 Example of mean, median and range 73

  4.3 Correlation 78

  4.4 Simple linear regression 83

    4.4.1 Example of simple linear regression 83

  4.5 T-tests 86

  4.6 Chi-square 89

  4.7 Summary 92

5 Data for Python and data manipulation 93

  5.1 Basic data types in Python 93

5.1 The Data for chapter 5 94

5.3 Data manipulation 97

    5.3.1 Equal to 97

    5.3.2 Further expressions 99

    5.3.3 Exercise 5.1: basic commands 102

    5.3.4 Solution to exercise 5.1 102

    5.3.5 Characteristic variables 102

5.4 Data frame manipulation in Python 104

    5.4.1 Updating null values 104

    5.4.2 Creating new columns 106

    5.4.3 Where 107

    5.4.4 Exercise 5.2: creating a new column 111

6. Data merging 114

6.1 Creating the mock frame 114

6.2 Merging datasets 117

    6.2.1 Full/Outer join 118

    6.2.2 Exclusive joins 119

    6.2.3 Concatenating/appending data 121

    6.3 Summary 122

7 Analysis 123

7.1 Introduction to analysing data 123

    7.1.1 Creating the dataset 123

    7.1.2 Basic analysis 124

7.2 Summarising data by groups 124

    7.2.1 Example of summarising data by groups 125

7.3 Calculating percentages 127

    7.3.1 Example of creating percentages 127

    7.3.2 Exercise 7.1: summarising and percentages 130

7.3.3 Solution to exercise 7.1 130

7.4 Creating a simple management information (MI) report 131

7.4.1 Example of simple MI report 131

7.5 Exercise 7.2 creating a simple MI report using Python and Excel 136

7.5.1 Exercise 7.2: simple MI report 137

7.5.3 Solution to exercise 7.2 138

7.6 Summary 141

8. Simple linear regression in R 142

8.1 Introduction to regression 142

8.1.1 Recap of simple linear regression 142

8.1.2 Normal distribution 143

8.1.3 Calculating variance, standard deviation and standard error 144

8.1.4 Calculating simple linear regression 144

8.1.5 Calculating the linear regression 145

8.1.6 Calculating R-squared 147

8.1.7 Example of calculating the r-square 147

8.2 Python calculating simple linear regression 148

8.3 Exercise in Python- simple linear regression 149

8.3.1 Linear regression scenario 149

8.3.2 Python linear regression solution 150

8.4 Summary 152

9 Multiple linear regression 153

9.1 Multiple linear regression 153

9.1.1 Example of multiple linear regression 154

9.2 Creating a scored output file 156

9.3 The t-statistic 159

9.4 Exercise 9.2 162

9.5 Categorical variables in the model 166

- 9.5.1 Creating the dummy variables 166
- 9.5.2 Dummy variable trap 166
- 9.5.3 Example of categorical regression 167
- Summary 171

10 Logistic regression 172

- 10.1 Logistic explanation 172
- 10.2 Logistic model 173
  - 10.2.1 Creating a logistic model 173
  - 10.2.2 Example of creating a logistic model 173
- 10.3 Logistic measurements 179
  - 10.4.1 Gini (Somers' D) 179
- 10.4 Performance of initial logistic model 184
- 10.5 Creating a scorecard 186
  - 10.5.1 Exercise 10.1: logistic model 186
  - 10.5.1 Solution to exercise 10.1 187
- 10.6 Summary 194

11 Finale 195

Introduction

This book recognises that in everyday business, analysts use a mixture of software tools. This book is for the applied statistician/analyst/ decision scientist who has just started on their journey or needs complimentary material for their studying.

Using the application of work-through examples and screenshots, with clear instructions, this book has been designed to enable the reader in the use of Excel® and Python intelligently.

This book removes any presumption of previous skills/knowledge and covers the basics to empower the reader with a strong foundation in the application of statistics.

Additionally, this book also covers some advanced techniques in a clear and thought through manner, with examples and exercises.

The goal of this book is for the reader to carry out the exercises, to gain confidence in their work, pose the appropriate questions and provide solutions to workplace problems.

The material that compliments this book can be easily downloaded from www.drbrainstats.com.

1. Introduction to statistics

This chapter introduces the most common terminology used in statistics. Using Excel to calculate certain statistics, this will enable you to understand the calculations and how they are produced.

Excel is a very powerful analytical tool which can calculate many different statistics, as we will discover through this chapter and throughout this book.

This chapter provides an insight into statistics using Excel, covering many topics and provides a basis for the following chapters. The topics covered are:
- Averages
- Measurements
- Correlation
- Simple linear regression

All workings will be clearly shown and described to ensure an understanding of Excel and statistics is gained.

1.1 What is statistics?

The field of statistics is concerned with the collection, description, and interpretation of data. We can consider data as observed events, facts and figures. A typical statistic we may hear about every day is about the weather e.g.
- Higher than average rainfall for the month or,
- Hotter than average for the month

These statements require the averages from previous months to justify them. The next section details how we calculate insightful statistics for different scenarios.

1.2 Mean, median and mode

In statistics, there are three different types of averages:

- **Mean**

The result obtained by adding numbers together and then dividing this total by the count of numbers (normally people refer this figure to **average**)

- **Median**

The "median" is the "middle" value in the list of numbers. To find the median, using pen and paper, write the number listed in numerical order, then locate the middle one.

- **Mode**

The "mode" is the value that occurs most often. If no number is repeated, then there is no mode.

1.2.1 Example of mean, mode and median

Using Excel, we will calculate the mean (average), median and mode for the following list of values:

13, 18, 13, 14, 13, 16, 14, 21, 13

First, input the numbers in Excel, as shown in figure 1.1

Figure 1.1: List of numbers in Excel

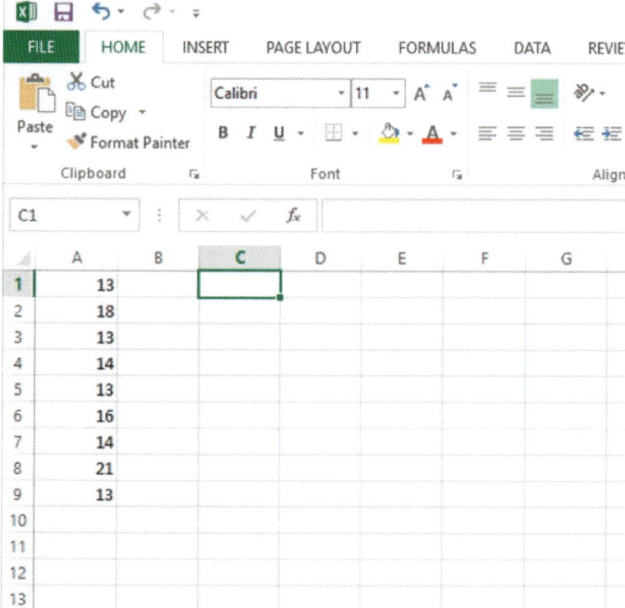

Next, in cell C1, input the word Average (in Excel they use 'average' instead of 'mean').

In cell C2, input the formula as shown

=AVERAGE(A1:A9)

This the equivalent of writing

=AVERAGE(A1,A2,A3,A4,A5,A6,A7,A8,A9)

In Excel, using ':' signifies that you want to include the cells in between those shown e.g. A1:A9 tells Excel to use the cells, A1, A2, A3, A4, A5, A6, A7, A8 and A9.

Figure 1.2: Average command in Excel

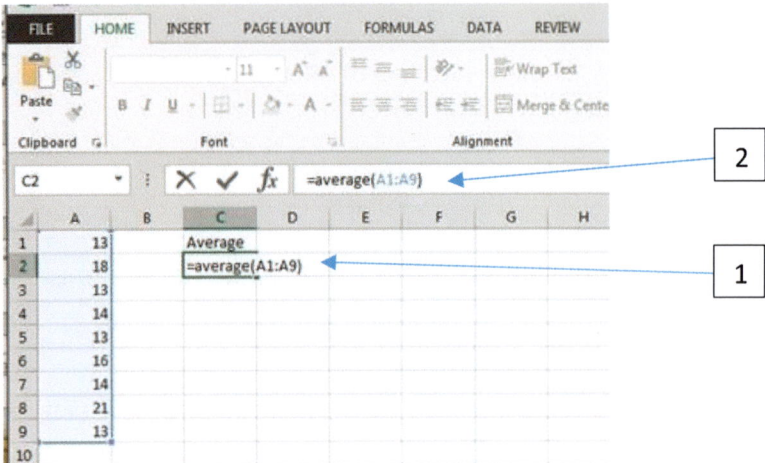

1) Write the formula in this cell (C2)
2) The formula is shown on this line (where you can also write the formula). This part of Excel is commonly known as the formula bar.

Then press enter

Figure 1.3: Average command in Excel

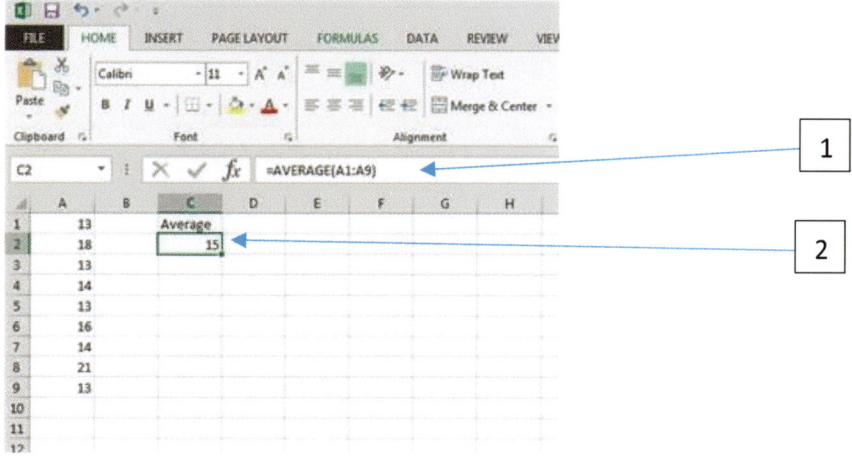

1) The formula is still shown in here
2) The result is shown here

As can be seen from figure 1.3, the average is 15.

Next, to calculate the median and mode we would use the following formulas

- Median

    =MEDIAN(A1:A9)

- Mode

    =MODE(A1:A9)

Figure 1.4: Results of average, median and mode in Excel

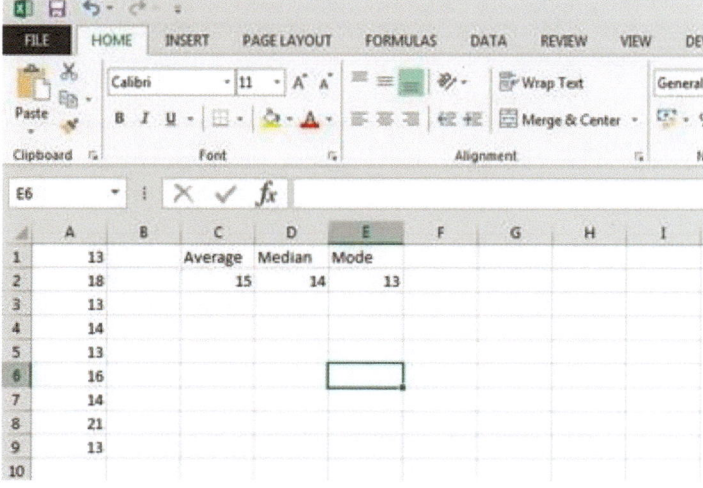

NOTE: The function 'mean' does not exist in Excel

1.3 Measurements

When dealing with statistics, we have to know the reliability of the figures produced. Using specific measurements, we can test if the figures produced can be used with 'confidence'. Excel allows us to calculate a range of measurements:

- Range: the difference between maximum and minimum figures

    =MAX (range) - MIN (range)

- Variance: the average of the squared differences from the Mean

    =VAR(range))

- Standard deviation: a common statistic as it provides a good indication of the variability of a set of data. However, it is not the best statistic to use when comparing different sets of data, especially if the data are of different sizes

    = STDEV(range)

- Standard error: provides an indication of the confidence of the mean. This is often used as an error measurement

    =STDEV (range) / SQRT (COUNT (range))

Figure 1.5: Range, variance, standard deviation and standard error in Excel

	A	B	C	D	E	F
1	13		Average	Median	Mode	
2	18		15	14	13	
3	13					
4	14					Commands used
5	13		Range	8		=MAX(A1:A9) - MIN(A1:A9)
6	16		Variance	8		=VAR(A1:A9)
7	14		Standard deviation	2.828427		=STDEV(A1:A9)
8	21		Standard Error	0.942809		=STDEV(A1:A9) / SQRT(COUNT(A1:A9))
9	13					

1.3.1 Exercise 1.1: measurements

The first exercise explores some simple fraud analysis. You ask two students to test a random group of students from the same class, 6 times and get their average test score results. You think one of the students did not carry out the exercise and fictionalised their results, while another one carried out the exercise as asked. The results were recorded in table 1.1

Table 1.1: Exercise 1.1 data

Data 1	Data 2
21.1	14.8
23.5	27.5
16.8	40.6
19.2	8.2
23.3	33.9
22.8	1.7

Copy the figures into Excel and calculate:
- Average
- Median
- Mode
- Range
- Variance
- Standard deviation
- Standard error

Using the different measurements, which dataset would we use with 'confidence' and are therefore not fictional?

1.3.2 Solution to exercise 1.1

Figure 1.6: Exercise1.1 solution

	A	B	C	D	E	F	G
1		Data 1	Data 2				
2		21.1	14.8				
3		23.5	27.5				
4		16.8	40.6				
5		19.2	8.2				
6		23.3	33.9				
7		22.8	1.7				
8						Formula used	
9	Average	21.11667	21.11667			=AVERAGE(B2:B7)	
10	Median	21.95	21.15			=MEDIAN(B2:B7)	
11	Mode	#N/A	#N/A			=MODE(B2:B7)	
12	Range	6.7	38.9			=MAX(B2:B7) - MIN(B2:B7)	
13	Variance	7.117667	233.5017			=VAR(B2:B7)	
14	Standard deviation	2.667896	15.28076			=STDEV(B2:B7)	
15	Standard Error	1.089164	6.238345			=STDEV(B2:B7) / SQRT(COUNT(B2:B7))	

From figure 1.6, data1 and data2 have the same average (mean) but, the other statistics associated with their data varies significantly. As data1 has a much lower variance, standard deviation and standard error, we would tend to trust these results rather than those in data2. Therefore, we could conclude that the data provided by student 2 was most probably fiction.

Additionally, since the numbers are not repeated the mode cannot be calculated thus, the '#N/A' shown in Excel.

1.4 Correlation

Correlation tells us whether two variables vary in synchrony, i.e. as one increase the other also increases (or decreases). The correlation statistic varies between 1 and -1:

- 1: perfect positive correlation, both figures increase or decrease together
- 0: no correlation, no pattern between the number
- -1: perfect negative correlation, as one figure increases the other decreases and vice-versa

As an exercise to demonstrate correlation we will be creating the perfect scenarios and zero correlation in Excel.

The Excel formula for correlation is:

=CORREL(*range1, range2*)

1.4.1 Example of correlation

Copy table 1.2 into Excel so that we can calculate the correlation between:
- data1 and data2
- data1 and data3
- data1 and data4

Table 1.2: Correlation data

Data 1	Data 2	Data 3	Data 4
1	10	100	55
2	20	90	55
3	30	80	55
4	40	70	55
5	50	60	55
6	60	50	55
7	70	40	55
8	80	30	55
9	90	20	55
10	100	10	55

Table 1.3: Correlation results

Comparing	Correlation	Formula
data1 and data2	1	=CORREL(A2:A11,B2:B11)
data1 and data3	-1	=CORREL(A2:A11,C2:C11)
data1 and data4	#DIV/0!	=CORREL(A2:A11,D2:D11)

From table 1.3:
- data 1 is perfectly positively correlated with data 2
- data 1 is perfectly negatively correlated with data 3
- data 1 and data 4 are not correlated at all, so Excel gives back an error. In this instance, the error code resembles 0.

The next part of this exercise involves two sections:
1. renaming a spreadsheet
2. producing graphs in Excel of the correlation data

This will be demonstrated using screenshots.

Figure 1.7: Renaming an Excel sheet

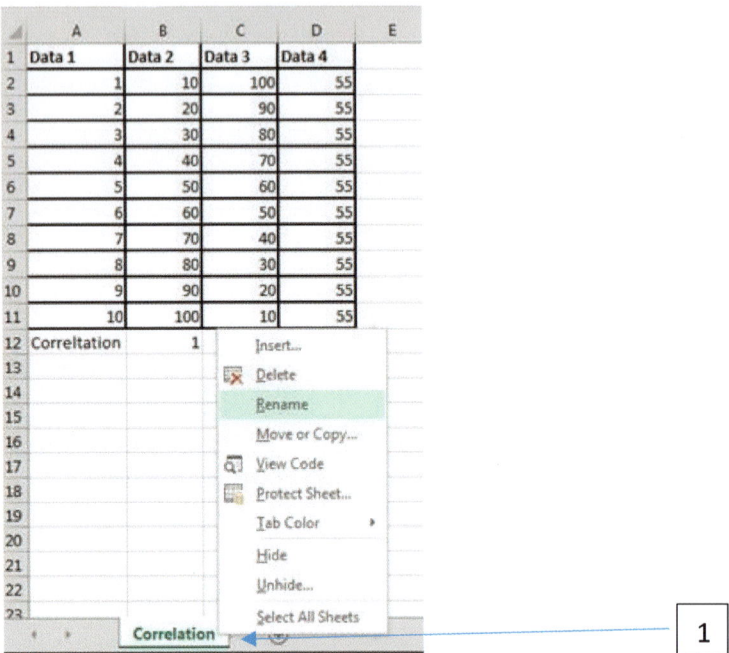

For ease of reference, this Excel sheet has been renamed to correlation.

1) Right-click in the box at the bottom
    a. Select Rename as highlighted
    b. Type Correlation

Renaming sheets in Excel is very simple and can aid you to locate key information easier.

Excel can provide insightful graphs with ease. In this example, we will be creating a very simple graph using the scatter graph function. Scatter graphs have more functionality than line graphs, which is the reason why we are using them here.

Figure 1.8: Creating a scatter graph

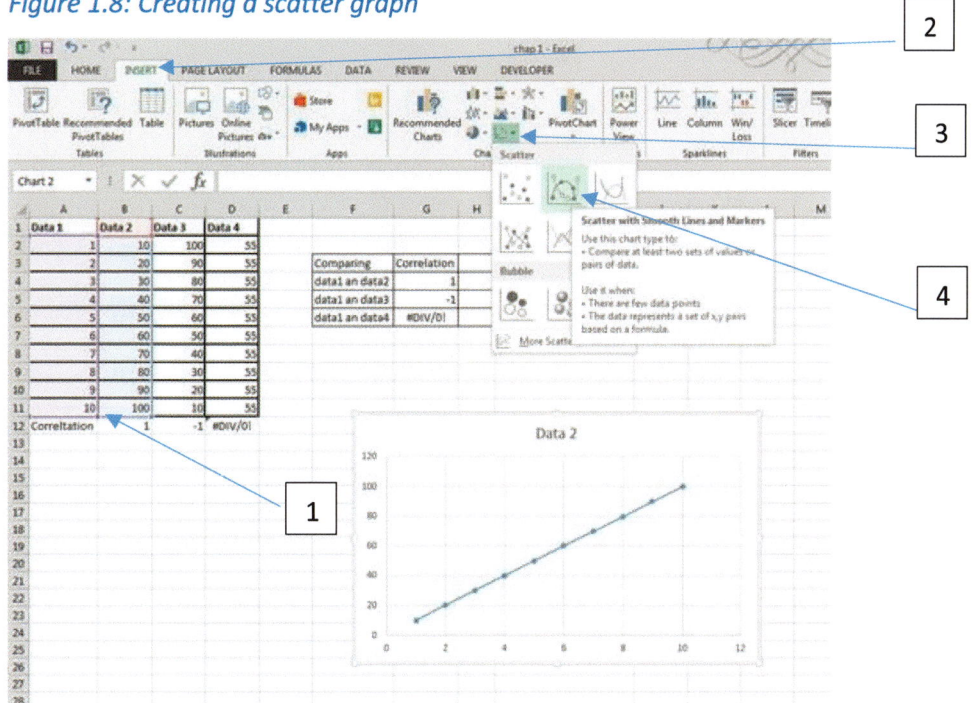

1) Highlight cells A1 to B11
2) Select the INSERT tab at the top of the screen
3) Click on scatter graph button
4) Select Scatter with smooth lines and markers

As we need to map data1 against data3 and data1 with data4, the following is required:
- Click on the graph just created with the mouse
- Right-click in the graph and click on **Select data** as shown in figure 1.8

Figure 1.8: Adding further plots in a scatter graph (1)

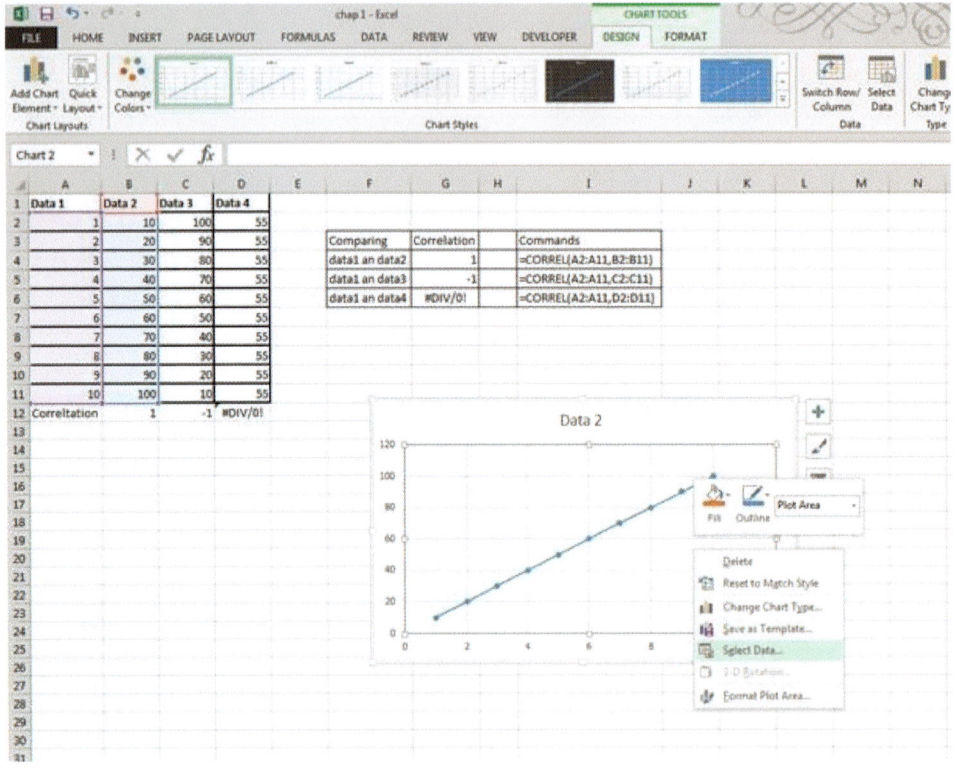

Figure 1.9: Adding further plots in a scatter graph (2)

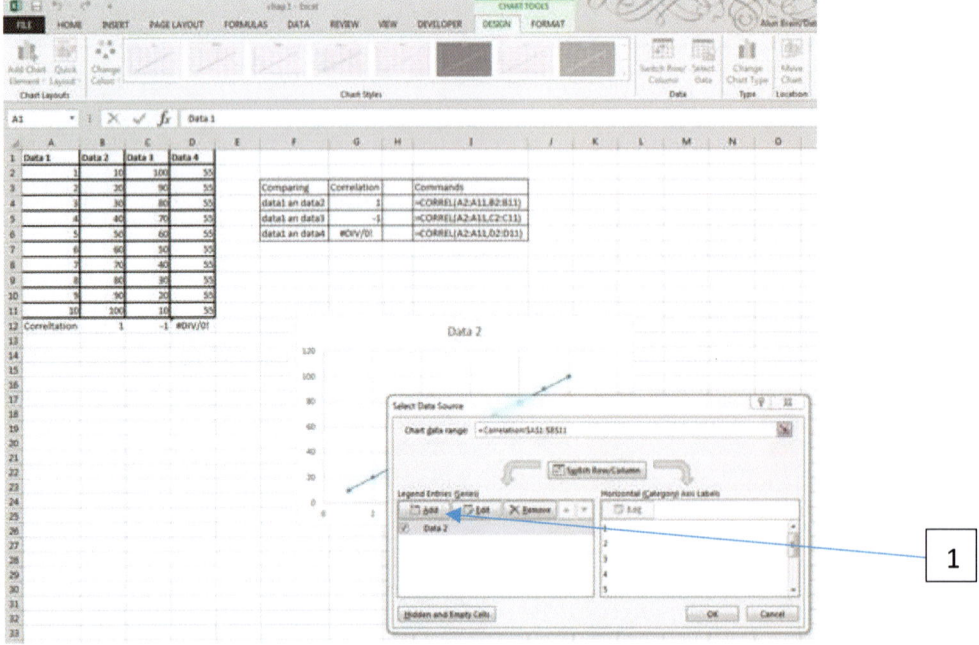

1) Click on Add

Figure 1.10: Adding further plots in a scatter graph (3)

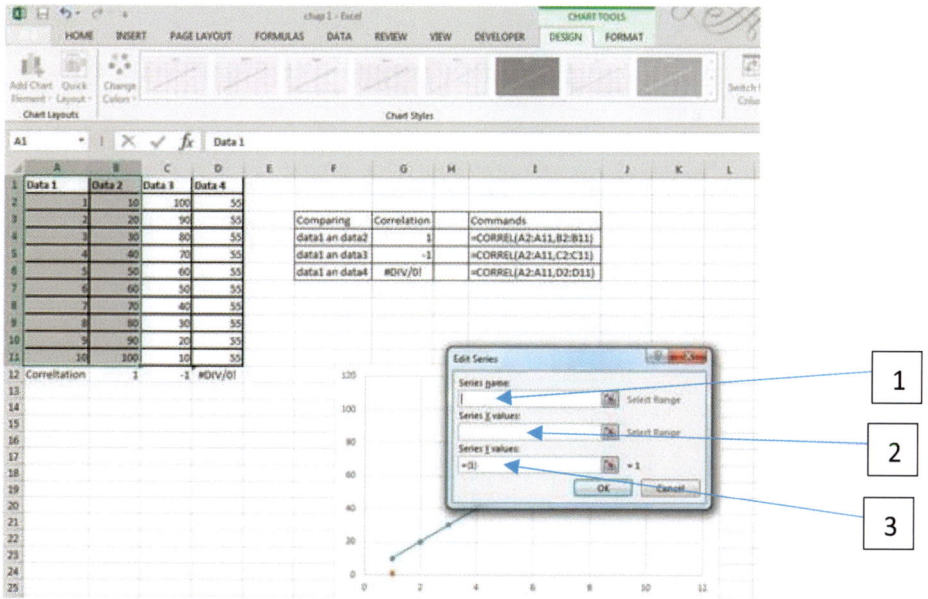

1) This is the name we want to give the line
    a. Data 3
2) The x-axis is the horizontal axis, so will need the data from data 1. Click in the box
    a. Highlight the cells A2 to A11
3) The y-axis is the vertical axis, so will need data from data 3. Click in the box
    a. Highlight the cells C2:C11

As you will notice, Excel will complete the required information

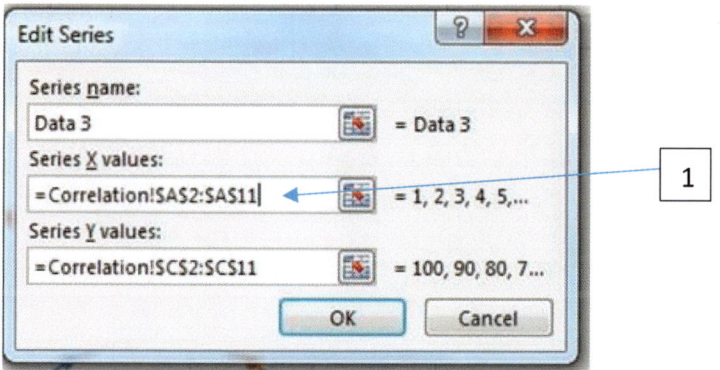

Click 'OK'

=Correlation!$A$2:$A$11

1) Deciphering this formula is as follows
   a. Correlation- the name of the sheet
   b. !- tells Excel that the name of the sheet is complete and expect cell references
   c. $A$2:$A$11- tells Excel that we use the cells A2 to A11.
      i. The $ tells Excel that this an *absolute cell reference*

Absolute cell references signify that if you copied this formula elsewhere, the cells nominated will not change.

Repeat the above for data 4, so we get

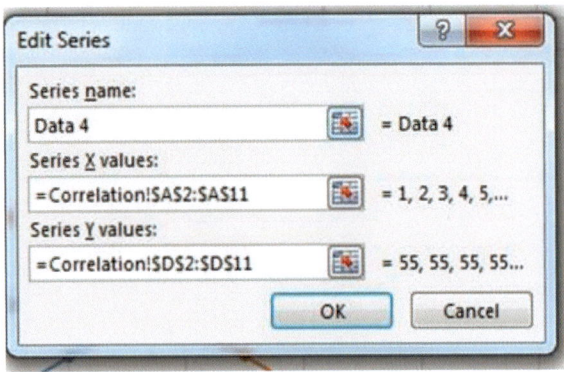

You should have produced a graph as shown in figure 1.11.

Figure 1.11: Correlation graphs

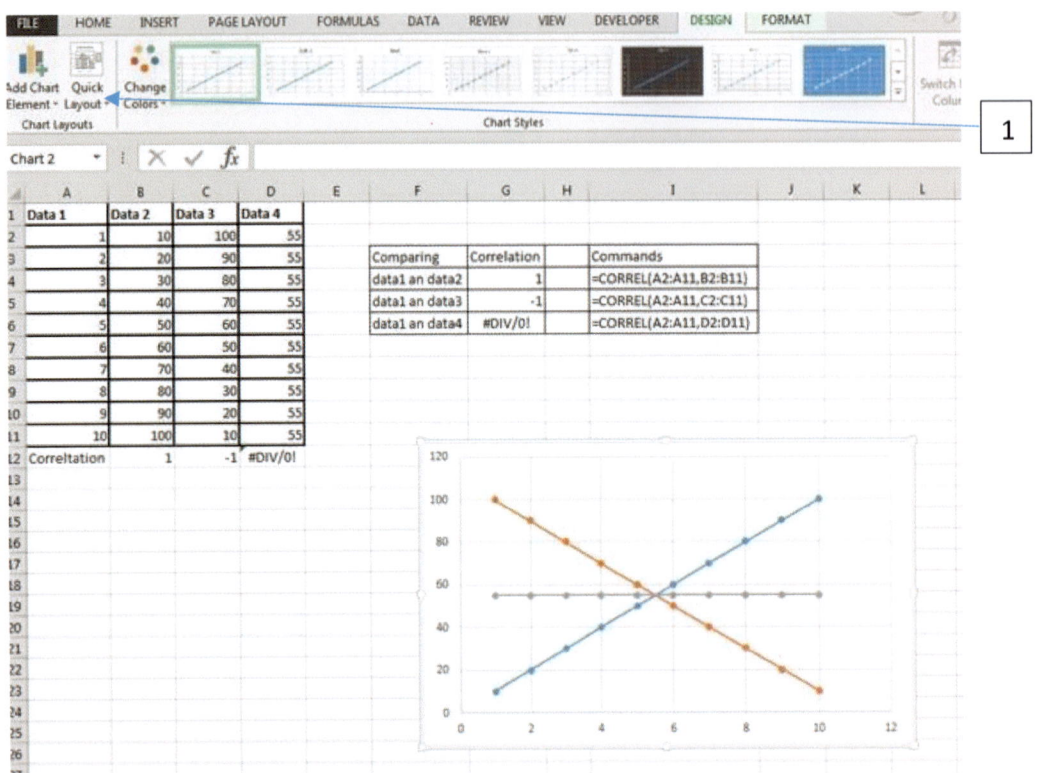

1) With the graph still highlighted, Click on the quick layout

Figure 1.12: Changing the appearance of a graph (1)

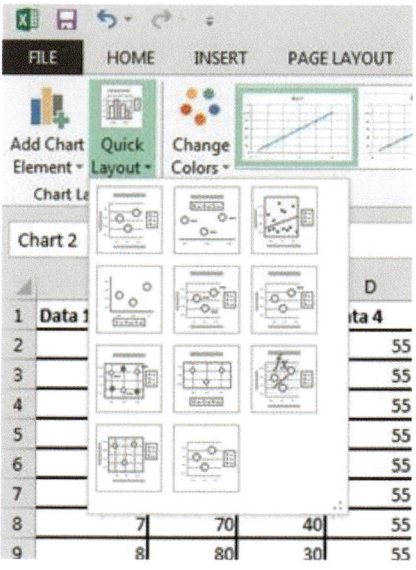

You get a variety of graphs to choose from, click the first one in the top left corner.

Figure 1.13: Changing the appearance of a graph (2)

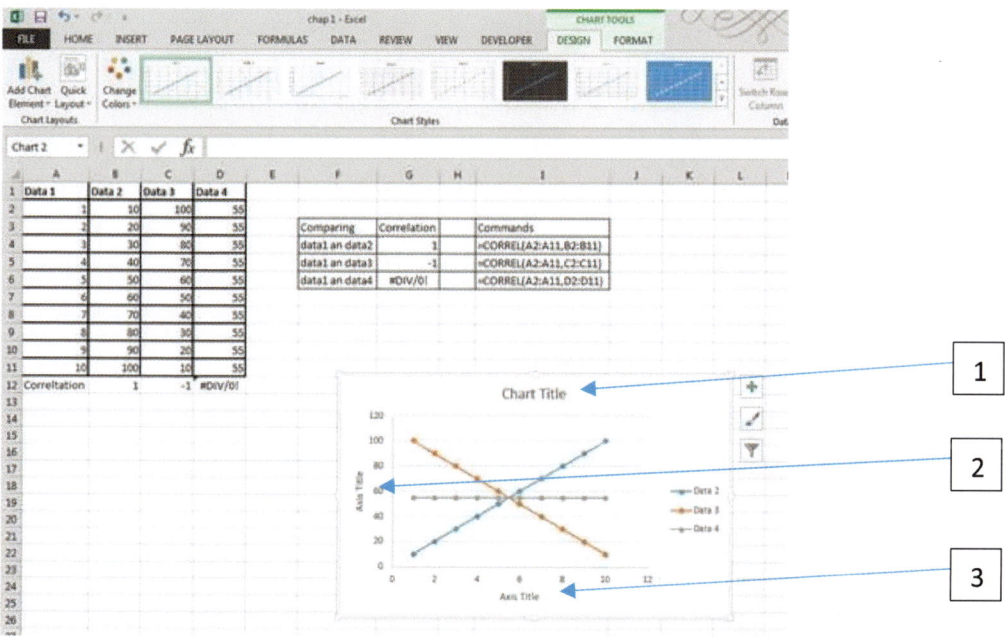

As you can see, we can now populate the graph with further information. This will involve using the mouse to click into the relevant part of the chart.

1) Click on Chart Title, to give the chart a name
    a. Correlation Plot

2) Click on 'Axis Title' on the y-axis (vertical).
   a. Numbers
3) Click on 'Axis Title' on the x-axis (horizontal).
   a. Data 1

Figure 1.14: Correlation plot

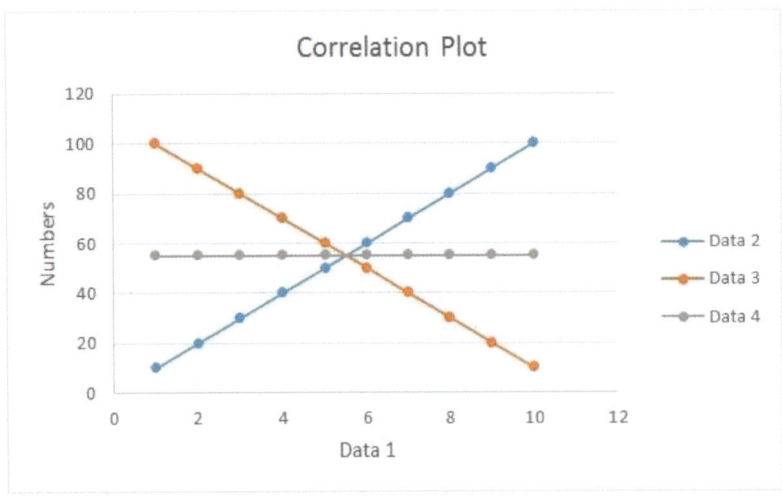

1.4.2 Exercise 1.2: correlation

This exercise requires calculating the correlation between intelligence and partners in a relationship. Table 1.4 contains test results, ranking out of 30, the intelligence of couples in a relationship. Is there a correlation between:

- Partner1 and partner 2
- Rank partner 1 and rank partner 2 (1=lowest 6=highest)

Table 1.4: Exercise 1.4 correlation data

Group	Partner 1	Partner 2	Rank partner 1	Rank partner 2
1	22.23	21.45	2	1
2	24.05	22.62	3	4
3	25.61	22.49	5	3
4	21.06	21.84	1	2
5	27.69	25.35	6	6
6	25.48	23.79	4	5

1.4.3 Solution to exercise 1.2

Figure 1.15: Correlation solution

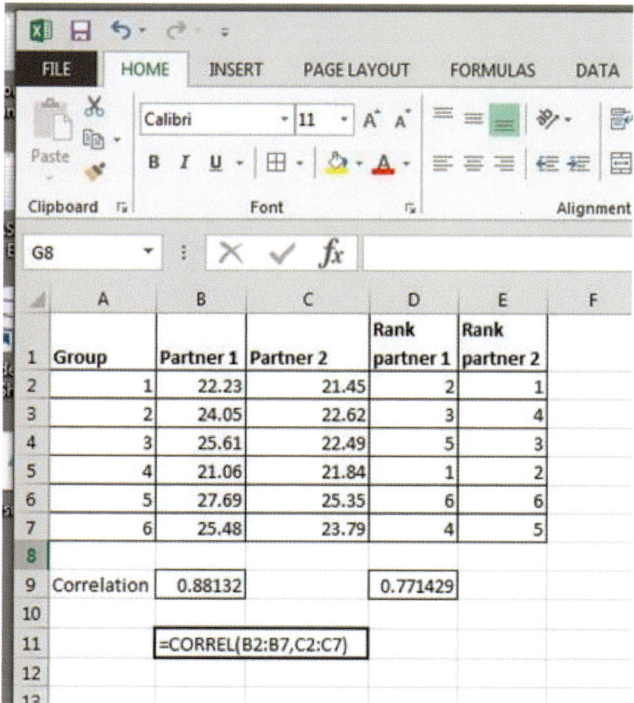

Figures above 0.7 or below -0.7 tends to imply correlation. Figure 1.15 shows us that there is a relationship between intelligence and partners, due to the correlation statistic being above 0.7.

Quick note, **correlation does not imply causation**. For example, in exercise 1.2, we cannot say that dating intelligent people causes intelligence.

1.5 Simple linear regression

Another common task in data analysis is to investigate the association between the two variables using regression.

Regression is used when we have reason to believe that changes in one variable causes changes in another. Correlation is not evidence for a causal relationship, but very often we are aware of a causal relationship and we design an experiment to investigate it further. The simplest kind of causal relationship is a straight-line relationship, which can be analysed using linear regression.

$$Y = mX + c$$

This fits a straight line to the data using the least squares method and gives the values of the slope (m) and intercept (c) that define the line.

There are several different methods of calculating the slope and intercept of a linear regression line in Excel, but the simplest method is to produce a scatter graph and use the 'Add Trendline' feature (as demonstrated next).

1.5.1 Example of simple linear regression

We want to test if there is a relationship between sponge thickness and its liquid absorbance. We have designed an experiment with different levels of sponge thickness, with the amount of liquid is absorbed. The results were recorded in table 1.5.

Table 1.5: Simple linear regression data

Sponge thickness (mm)	Absorbance (ml)
0.3	0.13
0.6	0.09
1.9	0.33
2.1	0.23
2.4	0.41
3.2	0.68
5.2	0.86
5.3	0.92
6	0.95
6.2	0.71
7.7	1.12

Copy the figures from table 1.5 into Excel and create a scatter graph (not joined), as shown in figure 1.16.

Figure 1.16: Scatter plot for simple linear regression

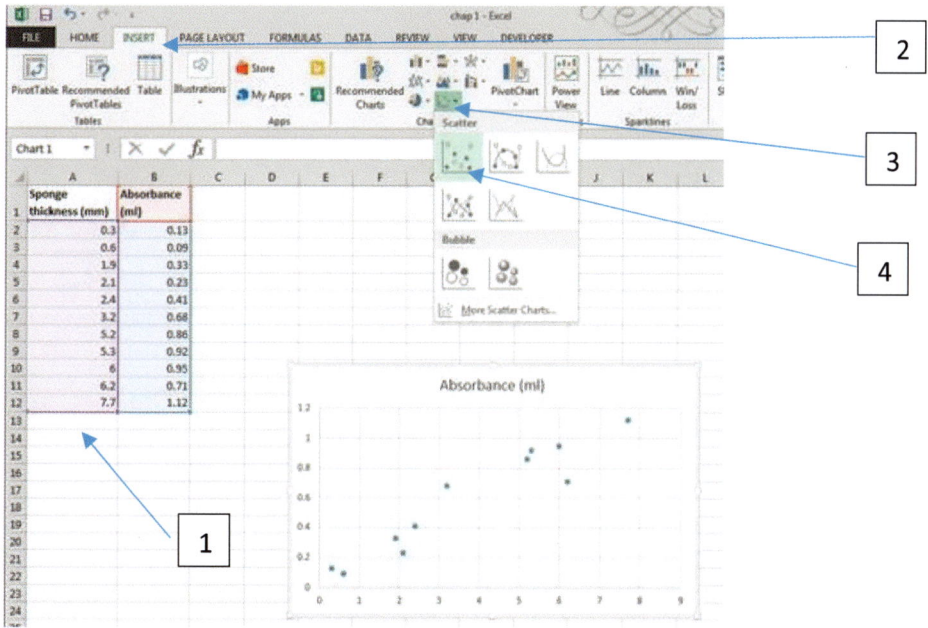

1) Highlight cells A1 to B12
2) Select the INSERT tab
3) Click on scatter graph button
4) Select Scatter, but this time, the first graph

To discover if there is a relationship between sponge thickness and absorbency, we perform the following.

Figure 1.17: Adding a trendline

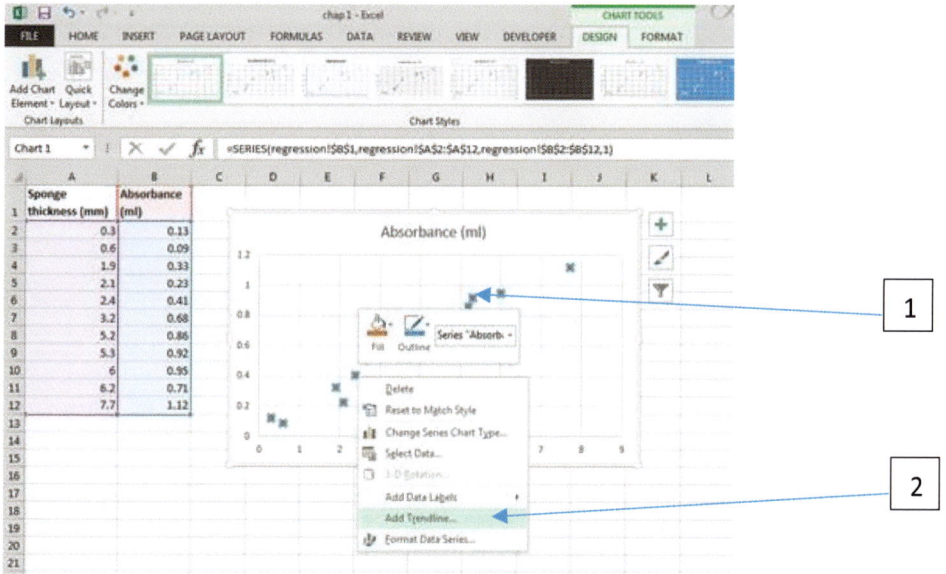

1) Right-click on any dot on the graph
2) A menu will pop up
    a. Click Add Trendline

Figure 1.18: Selecting equation and r-square

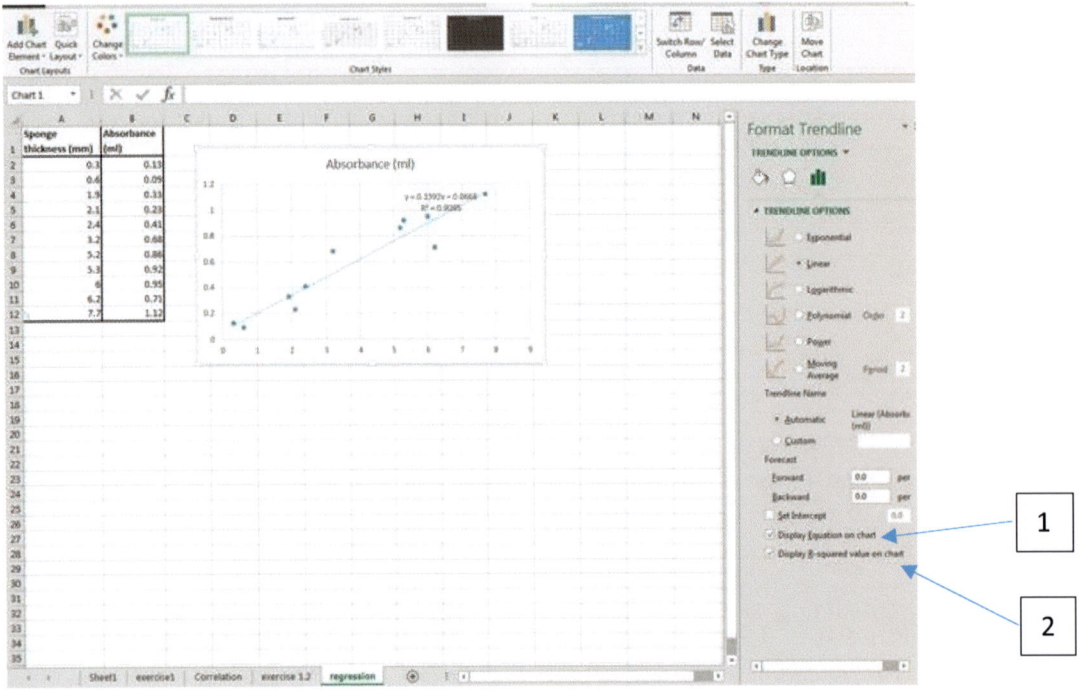

Within the menu selection tick the boxes for the following

1) Display Equation on chart
2) Display R-squared value on chart

The full equation of the slope and intercept values are now shown on the chart (as shown in figure 1.18)

Excel has produced a simple linear regression equation, which provides us insight into the relationship between sponge thickness and its absorbency.

$$Y = mX + c$$

The above equation represents a simple linear regression where

- Y is what we are trying to predict
- M is gradient (the value we times the 'X' value)
- X will be sponge thickness
- C is the intercept (where the line crosses the y-axis)

Using the quick layout function (as described in figure 1.13), the graph has been labelled as shown

- Title: simple linear regression graph
- X-axis: Sponge thickness (mm)
- Y-axis: Absorbance (ml)

Figure 1.19: Simple linear regression graph

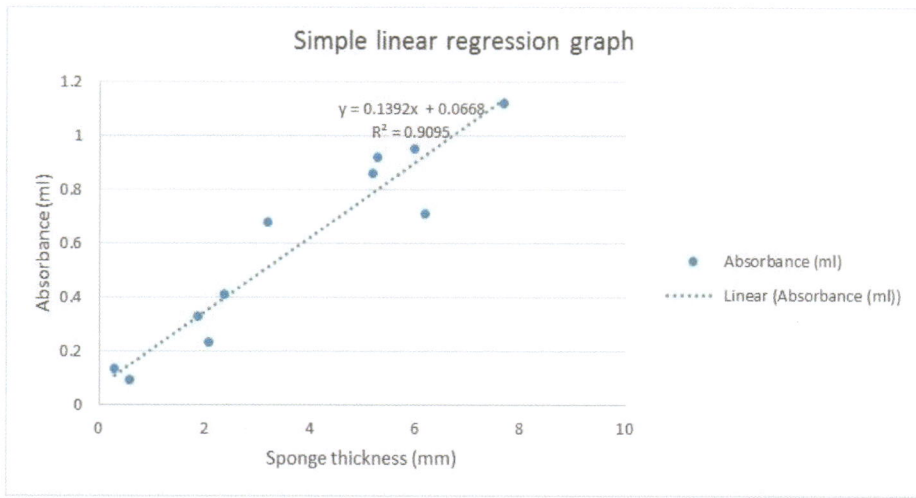

The straight line plots the relationship between the y-axis (absorbance) and the x-axis (sponge thickness).

Replacing the m and c in the above equation produces:

$$Y = 0.1392*X + 0.0668$$

For every mm of thickness, we should expect it to absorb 0.1392ml more substance (plus 0.068 ml). If someone asked, "How much absorbency should we expect from a sponge that is 10mm thick", we can provide the answer.

Using Y=mX + C, we know that:

- M = 0.1392
- C = 0.0668
- X = 10

$$Y = 0.1392*X + 0.0668$$
$$= 0.1392 * 10 + 0.0668$$
$$= 1.4588$$

If the sponge was 10mm thick, then we can expect it to absorb 1.4588ml. This demonstrates how we use equations to predict an outcome. E.g. for a sponge 50mm thick, we would expect it to absorb 7.028ml of liquid.

Before we have our Eureka moment of discovering a relationship between sponge thickness and absorbency rates, we have to measure the accuracy of this equation. This is why we ticked the box for the r-square value.

What is R-squared?

Put simply

$$r^2: \text{a measure of goodness-of-fit of linear regression}$$

The value r^2 is a fraction between 0.0 and 1.0 and has no units.

An r^2 value of 0.0 means that knowing X does not help you predict Y. There is no linear relationship between X and Y, and the best-fit line is a horizontal line going through the mean of all Y values.

When r^2 equals 1.0, all points lie exactly on a straight line with no scatter. Knowing X lets you predict Y perfectly.

An R-square value over 0.7 signifies a good fit.

Figure 1.20: R-square plots

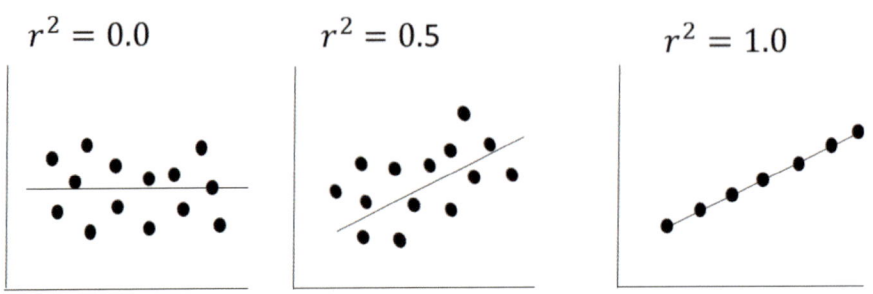

From the graph shown previously (figure 1.19), we have seen that the regression model produced an r-square value of 0.9095. This means the model predicts the absorbance rate good enough for us to use the model.

How to manually calculate a simple linear regression and r-square will be demonstrated in chapter 8. Currently, this book is designed to provide you with a hands-on experience and how to use different tools in Excel.

1.5.2 Exercise 1.3: simple linear regression

This exercise wants to discover if there is a relationship between age and eyesight. Table 1.6 contains data detailing eye-sight failure and age. Use this data to create a simple linear model that predicts sight failure rates from age. Additionally, can we use the model with confidence?

Table 1.6: Exercise 1.3 data

Age	Sight failure
22	7.2
6	1.8
93	13.4
62	8.8
84	14.4
14	4.8
52	6.6
69	12.2
104	13.2
100	16
41	9.4
85	12
90	10.2
27	2.8
18	6.4
48	4.2
37	10.8
67	14
56	13.4
31	8.4
17	7.8
7	5
2	1.2
53	9.4
70	11
5	1.4
90	13.8
46	8.4
36	7.8
14	1.8

Hint:

Create your scatter plot, right click on a dot, choose Add Trendline and tick the required boxes

1.5.3 Solution to exercise 1.3

Figure 1.21: Linear chart for exercise 1.3

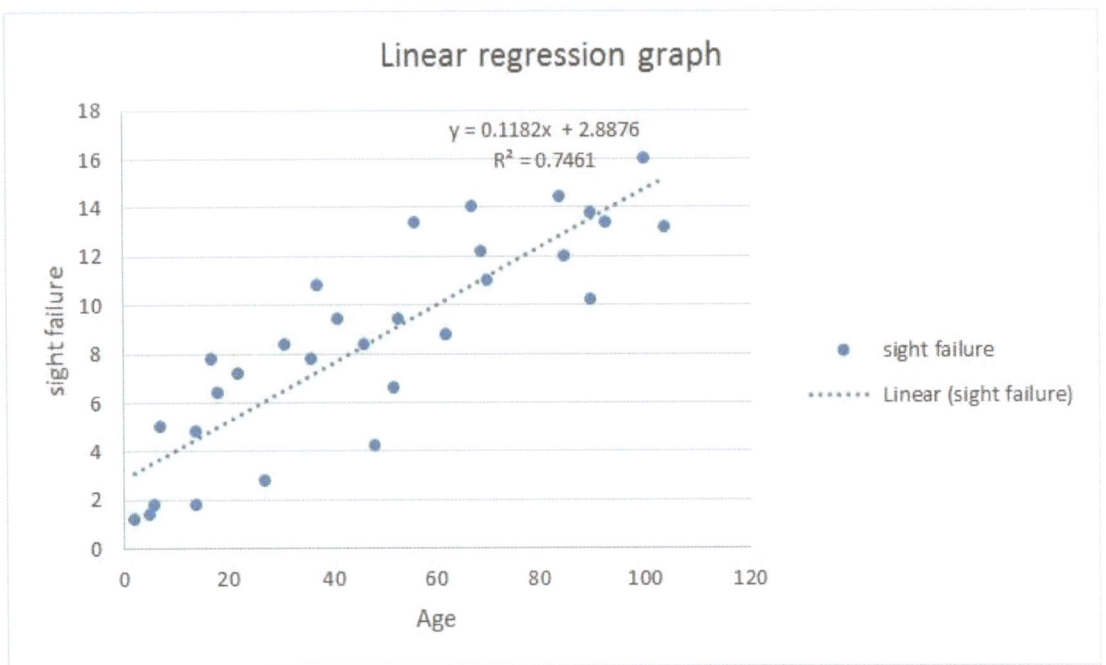

From figure 1.20, it can be observed that as age increases we expect to failure rates to increase by 0.1182 % as age increases.

With an r-square of 0.7461, we can use this model with confidence.

1.6 Summary

This chapter lays down the basics of statistics in an applied manner. This book has been designed to spend more on application than theory. In my experience, I have found Excel as the perfect tool to teach the application of statistics, due to its flexibility and its visibility. In Excel, it is difficult to hide your results and your calculations which is why I like to use it as a teaching tool whenever possible.

2. Further statistical exploration

This chapter aims to develop a deeper statistical understanding within Excel. Using plenty of examples and exercises, this chapter will build up your statistical knowledge within different scenarios.

This chapter will cover the topics:
- Distribution
- Null hypothesis
- T-tests
- Chi-square
- Chi-square test of association

Sections 2.1 to the beginning of 2.3 introduces some common terminology used in statistics, then we start on the fun from 2.3.1.

2.1 Distribution

Whenever we look at statistics we have to consider the distribution. Majority of the times the distribution will be focussed around the mean; this is referred to as a normal distribution.

What is a Normal Distribution?
A normal distribution is a continuous distribution that is "bell-shaped". Normal distributions can estimate probabilities over a continuous interval of data values. In a normal distribution the mean, median and mode are the same.

Below is an example of a perfect normal distribution plot.

Figure 2.1: Normal distribution plot

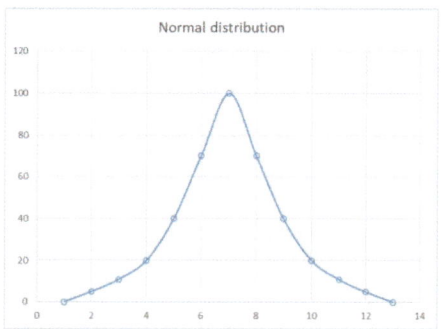

What are Skewed Distributions?

Skewed distributions are not symmetrical, but have their peak either to the left or right of the distribution. Depending on where the peak is, determines the type of skewed distribution.

Figure 2.2: Positive skewed distribution   *Figure 2.3: Negative skewed distribution*

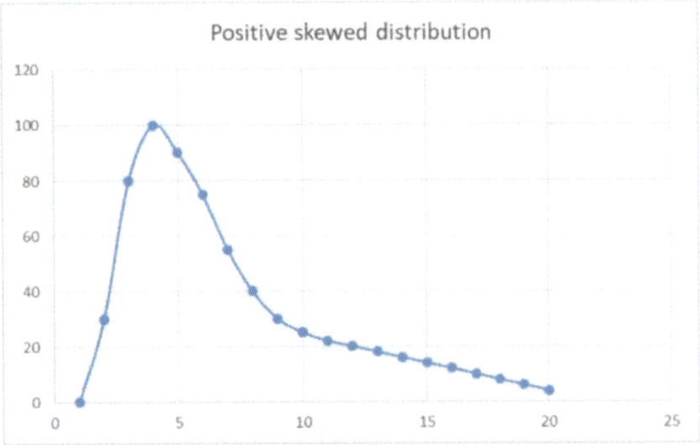

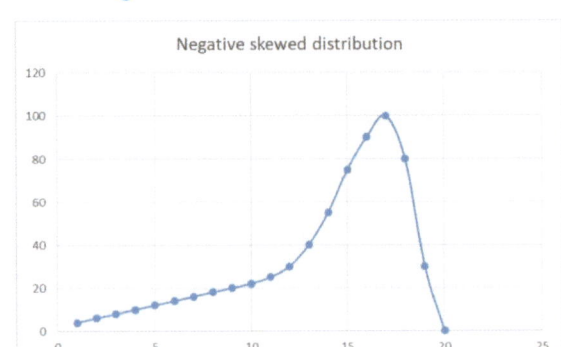

The figures attached to the graphs are nonsensical and are for illustration purposes only.

2.2 Null hypothesis

The null hypothesis states that there is no relationship between two measured occurrences. As a statistician, you need to disprove this hypothesis and discover a relationship.

Example of null hypothesis statement could be:
- There is no relationship between age and eyesight performance
- There is no relationship between tooth decay and toothache

The null hypothesis proposes the opposite we want to prove.

Conducting certain statistical tests, we can calculate a probability (**P**) to determine whether we can prove or disprove the null hypothesis. As a general rule, if **P** is less than 0.05 (5%) then we can say that there is a significant probability that the occurrence did not occur by chance, so we can reject the null hypothesis. **P** calculates the probability of the occurrence happening by chance.

2.3 T-tests

One of the most common comparative statistical tests used is called the *t*-test. This is used when there are just two sets of normally-distributed data to compare. In Excel, this is calculated using the formula

> =TTEST (range 1, range 2, tails, type)

This returns *P* directly (not the *t* statistic itself, which is not reported and which we don't need). As can be seen in the Excel formula above, two new statistical terms have been introduced:

- Tails
- Type

Tails

The tail test depends on the distribution of the data. By choosing one side, you are only interested in one part of the distribution (either the very lowest or the very highest). For two tail we are interested in all the population distribution

Figure 2.4: Two-tailed verses one-tailed hypothesis

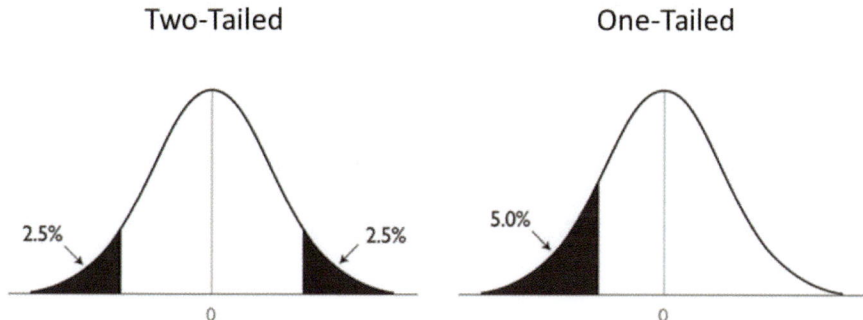

Tails can be 1 for a one-tailed test or 2 for a two-tailed test. Generally, we use the two-tailed test, which tests for differences regardless of sign (negative or positive numbers).

Type

There are three types of T-tests available in Excel. Suppose you wanted to test whether plant growth would increase after moving into a green-house or breathe rate increased after running up a hill. In these cases, you would be comparing the breathing rate of the same people or the growth of the same pot of plants before and after the greenhouse. This would require a "paired" or "dependent" T-test. Excel calls this a "type 1" test.

Let's look at another situation. Suppose you want to know whether arts students sleep more than science students. You would then have two groups of test subjects, each unique in their group (you would not take 2 measurements on each person). For this scenario, you would use an "unpaired" or "independent" t-test. Excel calls these "type 2" or "type 3" tests. Now the tricky part is to decide which of these two tests to use. Are the standard deviations about the same for both groups, or are they different? You can test this statistically, but if in doubt use "type 3" for unequal variance paired data (where the sets are from different individuals), and both are common.

2.3.1 Example of t-test

In this example, we want to test the effectiveness of a new drug. You ask a random selection of students their well-being (score 0 to 20), then without telling them, you start giving them an untested drug. After a week you ask the same people their well-being. The results were recorded as shown in table 2.1.

Table 2.1: Example 2.1 data

Well-being pre-treatment	Well-being post-treatment
3	5
0	1
6	5
7	7
4	10
3	9
2	7
1	11
4	8

For the exercise, answer the following:

1. What is your null hypothesis?
2. Calculate the mean & standard deviation
3. Are they correlated?
4. Calculate the t-test value to monitor if there has been a difference in the student's well-being.

Solution to the example of t-tests

1) Null Hypothesis

There is no relationship between the drug and better well-being

2)

Figure 2.5: T-Test results

	Well-being pre-treatment	Well-being post-treatment
Average	3.3333	7.0000
Standard deviation	2.2361	3.0414
Correlation	0.1470	
t-test	0.0137	

Formula
=TTEST(B2:B10,C2:C10,2,1)

3) The two datasets are not correlated.
4) For the t-test, we would use a two-tailed type (2). As we are using the same people in the experiment, post and pre-drug treatment, this requires a type 1 test, as shown in figure 2.1. From the t-test result, we can determine that the chance of this number occurring by chance alone (given the null hypothesis) is about .014 (or 1.4%)

To word the results statistically….

We reject the null hypothesis in favour of the alternative. Only once or twice out of every 100 times, if we repeated this experiment (and the null hypothesis was true) we would get a t-statistic of this size. Therefore, we conclude that it is more likely to have been due to some systematic, deliberate cause. If all other confounds are eliminated, this systematic cause must have been the drug.

Or in simpler terms, **the drug changed the students' well-being, positively**

2.3.2 Exercise 2.1: t-tests

In the next exercise, you have become a teacher and have been approached by a medicinal company to test a new drug that claims to enhance the intelligence of children. You split the class into 2 random sets, Group 1 takes the new drug with Group 2 being the control group (takes a placebo). Each group sits a test, then after 2 weeks of the children taking the drugs, the class sit a new test. The change in test scores was recorded as shown in table 2.2.

Table 2.2: Exercise 2.1 data

Group 1	Group 2
35	2
40	27
12	38
15	31
21	1
14	19
46	1
10	34
28	3
48	1
16	2
30	3
32	2
48	1
31	2
22	1
12	3
39	29
19	37
25	2

What is your null hypothesis? Use Excel to calculate the mean, standard deviation. Are they correlated? Are the results significant (what type would you use)?

2.3.3 Solution to exercise 2.1

1) Null Hypothesis

    The drug has no effect on children's intelligence

2)

Figure 2.6: Exercise 2.1 t-test results

	Group 1	Group 2
Average	27.15	11.95
Standard deviation	12.51	14.61
Correlation	-0.3959	
t-test	0.0011	

Formula

`=TTEST(A2:A21,B2:B21,2,3)`

3) The data is not correlated
4) For the t-test, we chose a two-tailed type (2), and as we are not using the same people in the experiment, this requires a type 3 test, as shown in figure 2.6. From the t-test result, we can determine that the chance of this number occurring by chance alone (given the null hypothesis) is about .0011 (or 0.11%)

On average a child's intelligence increases by 15.20 points.

The t-test produces a figure of 0.001 which means these results are very significant and can only happen by chance 0.1% of the times. Therefore, we can reject the null, the drug improved test scores.

2.4 Chi-square

So far we have only concerned ourselves with measurement data. Sometimes, the results are not measurements but counts (frequencies), such as the number of people who respond to a marketing mail campaign. With frequency data, you shouldn't use the *t*-test but use 'chi-squared' ($\chi 2$) test instead. Chi-square is used to compare frequency data in different categories with expected data.

Excel formula:

> =CHITEST (observed range, expected range)

This returns the probability **P** that the null hypothesis is true.

The **chi-square statistic** compares the observed to the expected observations **under the assumption of no association** between the row and column classifications

The chi-square statistic may be used to test the hypothesis of no association between two or more groups, populations, or criteria. If P is less than 5% then the data does not agree with the theory, and if P is greater than 5% then the data agrees with the theory).

2.4.1 Example of chi-square

We go for a walk in a lovely forest and comment on the colour of the apples. We expect to see ¾ red apples and ¼ green apples. After counting the apples in the forest, the results were recorded.

Table 2.3: Example for chi-square data

Apple Colour	observed
Red	545
Green	185
total	730

For chi-square, we test the actual results against what we expected, therefore we calculate the expected amount of apples for each colour. There are a total of 730 apples and we expect ¾ to be red and a ¼ green.

In Excel, the expected is easily calculated

Figure 2.7: Expected results for chi-square

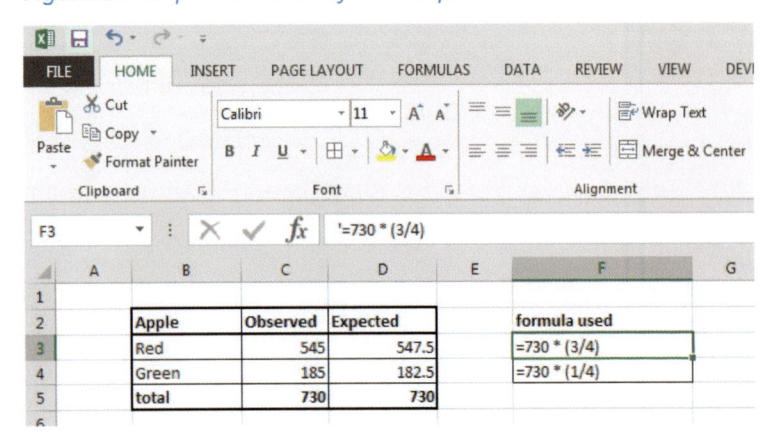

	Apple	Observed	Expected		formula used
	Red	545	547.5		=730 * (3/4)
	Green	185	182.5		=730 * (1/4)
	total	730	730		

F3: =730 * (3/4)

Now that we have the observed and expected figures, the chi-square statistic can be calculated in Excel.

Figure 2.8: Chi-square formula in Excel

Apple	Observed	Expected		formula used
Red	545	547.5		=730 * (3/4)
Green	185	182.5		=730 * (1/4)
total	730	730		
Chi-square		0.830791211		=CHITEST(C3:C4,D3:D4)

With a high chi-square value (above 0.05), we can say that our theory was correct. The observed is close to the expected, thus proving our theory.

NOTE: the reason why we use chi-square and not simple arithmetic, is to be certain that our results are significant and we can announce our results with confidence.

2.4.2 Exercise 2.2 chi-square

This next exercise uses marketing campaign statistics. A mailing campaign of 1000 letters split by 500 to males and 500 to females was conducted. We expect men to respond twice as likely as females. Therefore, for every 30 responses, we would expect 10 of these from women and 20 from men. The results were recorded as shown in table 2.4. Is our theory correct?

Table 2.4: Exercise 2.2 data

Postal	Observed
Male	120
Female	85

2.4.3 Solution to exercise 2.2

Figure 2.9: Chi-square solution for exercise 2.2

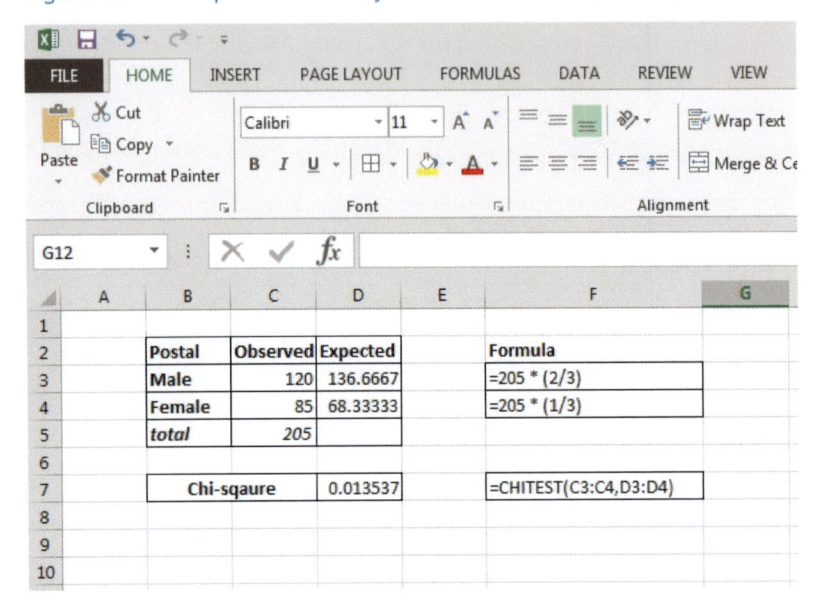

	Postal	Observed	Expected		Formula
	Male	120	136.6667		=205 * (2/3)
	Female	85	68.33333		=205 * (1/3)
	total	205			
	Chi-sqaure		0.013537		=CHITEST(C3:C4,D3:D4)

With a chi-square value of less than 0.05, our hypothesis was wrong, men do not represent two-thirds of the mailing response.

NOTE: As mentioned previously, we use chi-square statistics to enable us to announce our results with confidence.

2.5 Chi-square test of association

The chi-square test can also be used to investigate associations between frequency data in two separate groups. This is called the chi-squared test of association. The expected data are calculated by assuming that the counts in one group are not affected by the counts in a different group.

In other words, we are testing whether there is an association between the two groups. If *P is less than* 5% then there is a significant association between the two groups, but if *P is more than* 5% then the two groups are independent.

2.5.1 Example of chi-square test of association

In this scenario, we will be considering another marketing campaign. Questions were asked if the time of day affected the marketing campaign response. As before, we measured the response (observed), but for the expected, we have to calculate the expected by using totals (as shown in figure 2.10).

Figure 2.10: Chi-square test of association data

	A	B	C	D	E	F	G
1							
2			Promotion 1	Promotion 2	Promotion 3	Promotion 4	total
3		Morning	99	83	21	67	270
4	Observed	Afternoon	21	54	104	51	230
5		Total	120	137	125	118	500
6							
7		Morning	64.8	73.98	67.5	63.72	270
8	Expected	Afternoon	55.2	63.02	57.5	54.28	230
9		Total	120	137	125	118	500
10							
11							
12		formula for expected					
13		Morning	=C5 * 270 / 500	=D5 * 270 / 500	=E5 * 270 / 500	=F5 * 270 / 500	
14		Afternoon	=C5 *230 / 500	=D5 *230 / 500	=E5 *230 / 500	=F5 *230 / 500	

Figure 2.11: Chi-square test of association results

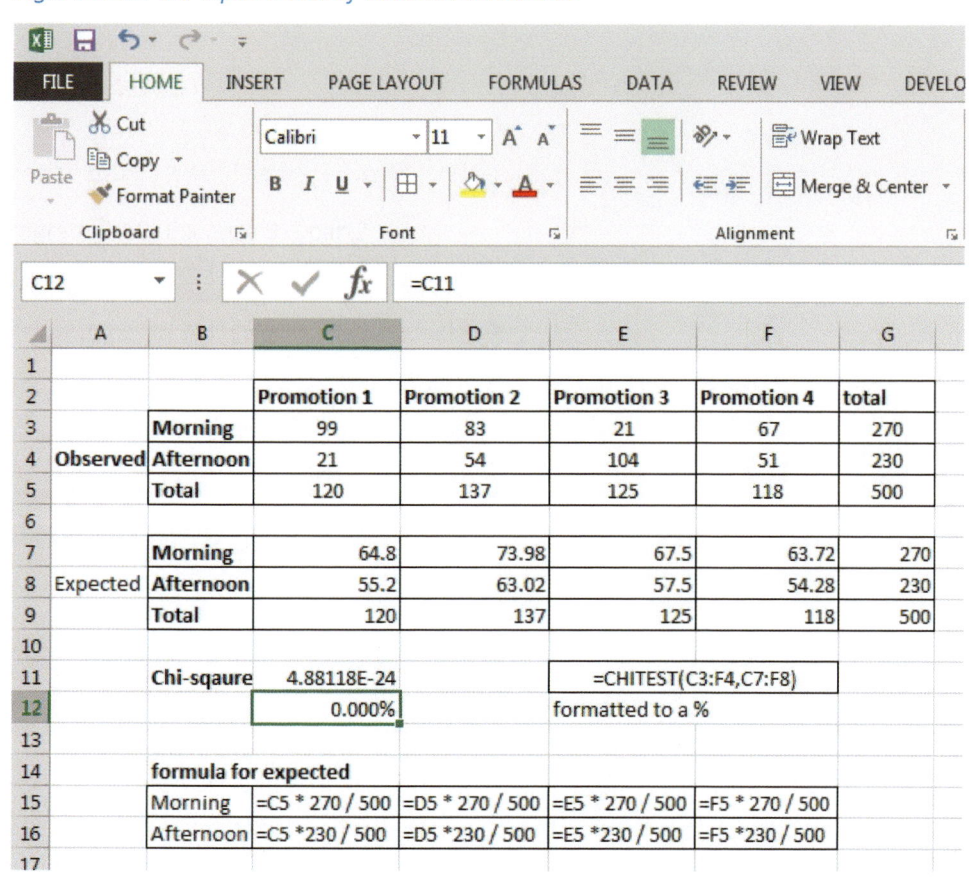

	A	B	C	D	E	F	G
1							
2			Promotion 1	Promotion 2	Promotion 3	Promotion 4	total
3		Morning	99	83	21	67	270
4	Observed	Afternoon	21	54	104	51	230
5		Total	120	137	125	118	500
6							
7		Morning	64.8	73.98	67.5	63.72	270
8	Expected	Afternoon	55.2	63.02	57.5	54.28	230
9		Total	120	137	125	118	500
10							
11		Chi-sqaure	4.88118E-24		=CHITEST(C3:F4,C7:F8)		
12			0.000%		formatted to a %		
13							
14		formula for expected					
15		Morning	=C5 * 270 / 500	=D5 * 270 / 500	=E5 * 270 / 500	=F5 * 270 / 500	
16		Afternoon	=C5 *230 / 500	=D5 *230 / 500	=E5 *230 / 500	=F5 *230 / 500	

With such a low chi-square value (less than 5%) we can assume that there is a strong relationship between time of day of sending out emails and promotions.

2.6 Summary

The main goal of this chapter is to demonstrate that in statistics, there's typically more than one way to conduct the analysis you require. When first starting statistics, people have always questioned the null hypothesis and have wondered why we are trying to prove the opposite, so I point them to the 'alternative hypothesis', which is the opposite of the null hypothesis.

3. Data mining in Excel

Data mining is a very powerful tool that can locate 'nuggets' of insightful information to enable decision makers to formulate strategies. There are many data mining strategies and tools available, but for this book, we will be concentrating on decision trees.

This chapter builds on the previous chapters to enable us to proceed to the next level. This chapter will cover the following:

- Understanding why we use decision trees
- How to use Chi-square statistics productively and intuitively
- Creating decision trees
- Delivering key findings from decision trees

3.1 Decisions trees

Decision trees display the mapping of complex behaviour into a simple diagram. Using a combination of statistical tools and common sense, simple rules can be created to provide key insight. They are mainly used to create rules for a binary (dichotomous) outcome e.g. yes/no.

3.1.1 Definitions

Figure 3.1 contains an image of a simple decision tree. Thirty people were surveyed outside a DIY store asking them what factors they would consider for completing their task during the day. The results were presented in a decision tree

Figure 3.1: Example of a decision tree

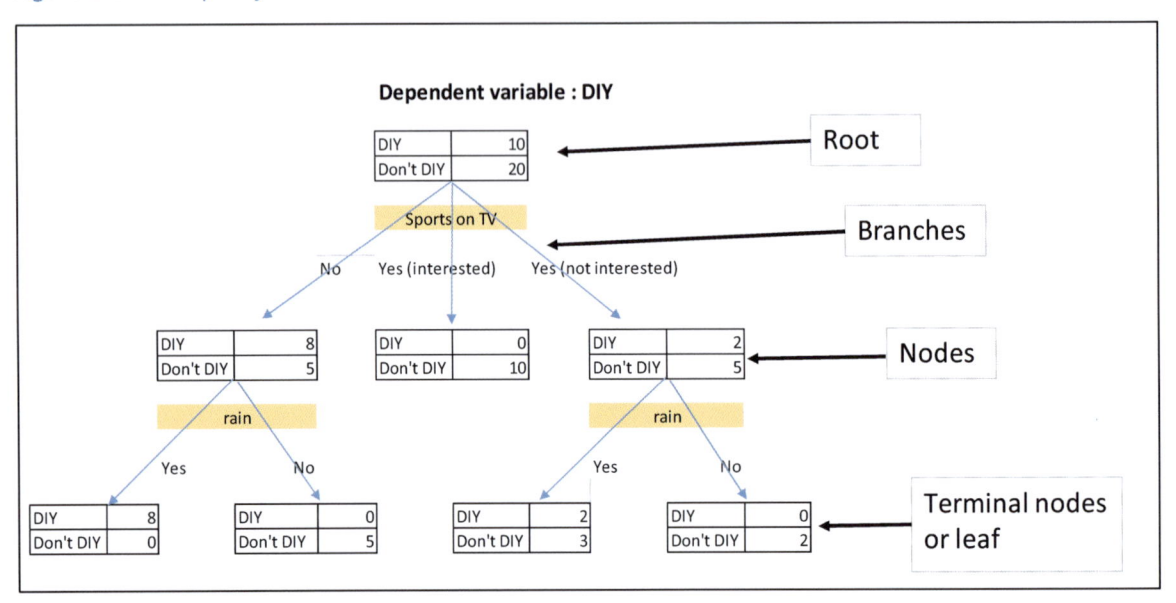

![Decision tree diagram showing Dependent variable: DIY at the root with DIY=10, Don't DIY=20. Branches split on "Sports on TV" into No, Yes (interested), Yes (not interested). The No branch leads to a node with DIY=8, Don't DIY=5, which splits on "rain" into Yes (DIY=8, Don't DIY=0) and No (DIY=0, Don't DIY=5). The Yes (interested) branch leads to DIY=0, Don't DIY=10. The Yes (not interested) branch leads to DIY=2, Don't DIY=5, which splits on "rain" into Yes (DIY=2, Don't DIY=3) and No (DIY=0, Don't DIY=2). Labels point to Root, Branches, Nodes, and Terminal nodes or leaf.]

Using the decision tree in figure 3.1, people who are interested in a specific sport are not likely to do DIY. For those people who did not realise there was sport on TV (no), then the weather was a major factor.

Decision trees can create a story which is simple to follow and understand.

The key terminology used are as follows:

- **Dependent variable**: the target variable, the root
- **Independent / explanatory variable**: the variables that create the rules
- **Continuous variable**: a numerical based variable (e.g. age/salary)
- **Categorical variable**: a character based variable (e.g. region)
- **Ordinal variable:** An ordinal variable is similar to a categorical variable. The difference between the two is that there is a clear ordering of the variables.
- **Bins**: what the categorical variable is split into (e.g. sports on TV is split into no, yes (interested), yes (not interested)
- **Pruning**: Sometimes trees can contain too much detail. Thus we 'prune' the tree at an appropriate level. Usually, this is done by using common sense.

3.1.2 How do we decide the node?

As usual, there is more than one method to do anything in statistics, including decision trees. In this book, we will be using the CHAID method. CHAID stands for Chi-square Automatic Interaction

Detector (or Detection, depending upon the source consulted). As we already have an understanding of chi-square, it makes sense to use chi-square methodology to create the decision tree.

Chi-square statistics enables us to discover variables (categorical based) that provide strong discrimination between their different components (bins). The chi-square (X^2) statistic is used to investigate whether **distributions** of categorical variables differ from one another.

3.2 Converting a continuous variable into a categorical variable

Converting a numerical variable into characteristic is straightforward, we just have to calculate the 'best' bins. If we used guesswork, this may potentially create bins without 'targets', which would not enable us to carry out the chi-square statistic.

First, download the Excel workbook binary. This workbook details the sales of a product with basic customer characteristics. The next stage entails segmenting the continuous explanatory variables into equal sized proportions based on the target variable (not total observations), as will be demonstrated in exercise 3.1.

3.2.1 Exercise 3.1

The Excel workbook, binary, has a binary response variable called **sold**, which is equal to 1 if a sale has been made, and 0 otherwise. This workbook also contains three predictor variables:

- Income (continuous)
- Mortgage % (% of wages used to pay the mortgage) (continuous)
- Tier (customer rank) (categorical/discrete).

The variable **tier** takes on the values 1 to 4. Tiers with a rank of 1 have the highest prestige, while those with 4 have the lowest.

We want to know if there a population that we can target cost effectively?

First, convert the continuous variables into categorical variables, with an equal number of targets in each bin (segment). This requires creating a new spreadsheet with all of the columns, but only where the sold column =1.

Figure 3.2: Creating categorical variables (1)

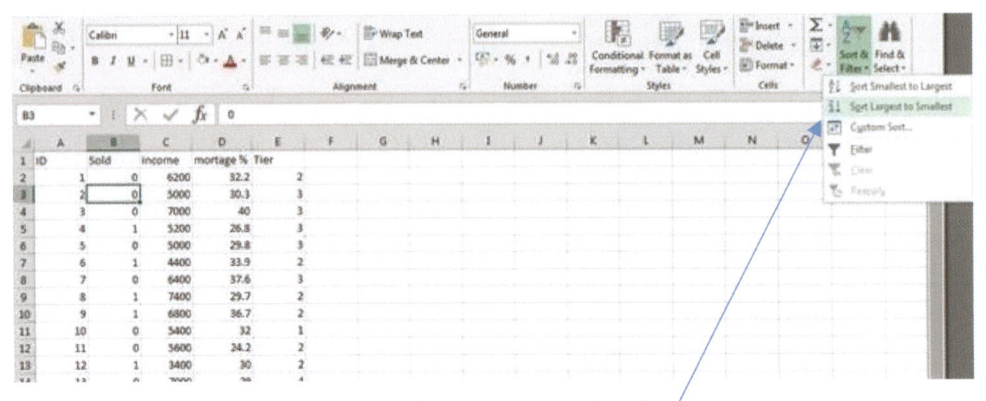

Sort the Excel spreadsheet by sold (Largest to Smallest).

Copy and paste all of the data where the sold flag = 1 into a new worksheet.

Figure 3.3: Snapshot of the Excel sheet where sold=1

There should be 89 customers where the sale flag =1.

The next stage requires producing 4 bins for income and mortgage. As we want each bin to have roughly the same number of targets, measure the values at each quarter. Sort this new sheet by **income.** At line 22, 44, 66 record these values.

- At line 22, income equals 5200
- At line 44, income equals 6000
- At line 66 income equals 6800

There is no need to know the last figure as any number above 6800 will represent our fourth and final bin.

Next, sort this new sheet by mortgage %. At line 22, 44, 66 record these values.
- At line 22, mortgage % equals 31.7
- At line 44, mortgage % equals 34.9
- At line 66 mortgage % equals 37.1

There is no need to know the last figure as any number above 37.1 will represent our fourth and final bin.

The next section details two methods for creating new columns with the bins.

3.2.2 Method1 of creating bins - copy and paste

The first method is the simplest but could be tiresome if we had data with over 10000 rows. First, sort the Excel sheet by income and in column F label it 'income group'. Populate this new column where appropriate:
- 5200 and under
- 5201 to 6000
- 6001 to 6800
- 6801 and above

Repeat for a new column called mortgage group
- 31.7 and under
- 31.8 to 34.9
- 35.0 to 37.1
- 37.2 and above

Accuracy is key when binning the columns income and mortgage %.

Figure 3.4: Creating the new bins using copy and paste

	A	B	C	D	E	F	G	H	I
1	ID	Sold	income	mortage	Tier	Income group	Mortgage group		
2	294	1	3000	28.4	2	5200 and under	31.7 and under		
3	12	1	3400	30	2	5200 and under	31.7 and under		
4	269	1	4000	31.5	2	5200 and under	31.7 and under		
5	103	1	4000	32.3	4	5200 and under	31.8 to 34.9		
6	6	1	4400	33.9	2	5200 and under	31.8 to 34.9		
7	225	1	4400	34.5	2	5200 and under	31.8 to 34.9		
8	29	1	4600	36.4	1	5200 and under	35.0 to 37.1		
9	263	1	4600	39.9	3	5200 and under	3.72 and above		
10	197	1	4800	26.2	2	5200 and under	31.7 and under		
11	292	1	4800	26.7	2	5200 and under	31.7 and under		
12	171	1	4800	29.1	1	5200 and under	31.7 and under		
13	175	1	4800	30.2	1	5200 and under	31.7 and under		
14	71	1	4800	37.1	4	5200 and under	35.0 to 37.1		
15	115	1	5000	31.3	2	5200 and under	31.7 and under		
16	33	1	5000	36	3	5200 and under	35.0 to 37.1		
17	4	1	5200	26.8	3	5200 and under	31.7 and under		
18	74	1	5200	31.9	3	5200 and under	31.8 to 34.9		
19	267	1	5200	33	2	5200 and under	31.8 to 34.9		
20	219	1	5200	36.5	4	5200 and under	35.0 to 37.1		

3.2.3 Method 2 of creating bins - If function

Excel If function

In Excel, we can use a function called 'If'. This allows you to create a value in one cell based upon a value (numeric or character) in a different cell.

=IF(logical_test, value_if_true, value_if_false)

- **Logical_test** is any value or expression that results in a TRUE or FALSE scenario e.g. if cell A2=3 is a logical expression. If the cell A2 equals 3, then this expression is **true**, else it is **false**
- **Value_if_true**: this is the value we want to be displayed if it is true. E.g. if the cell A2 equals 3, then we may want to display the text "A2 is 3".
- **Value_if_false**: this is the value we want to be displayed if it is false. E.g. if the cell A2 does not equal 3, then we may want to display the text "A2 is not 3".

Example

Copy the example as displayed in figure 3.5.

Figure 3.5: Example of an 'if' statement in Excel

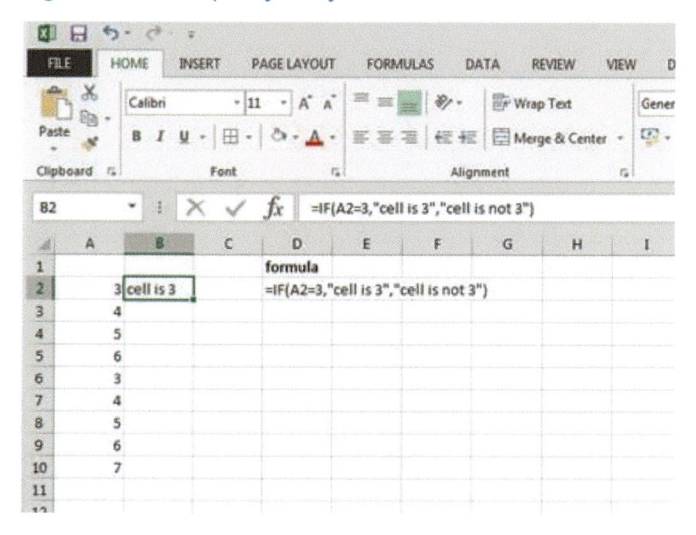

*formula cells are for reference only

Within the cell B3, is the formula

=IF(A2=3,"cell is 3","cell is not 3")

Shortcut to stop writing out multiple lines of formula

Instead of writing out this formula numerous times, we can use the 'drag' function.

Figure 3.6: Click and drag function in Excel (1)

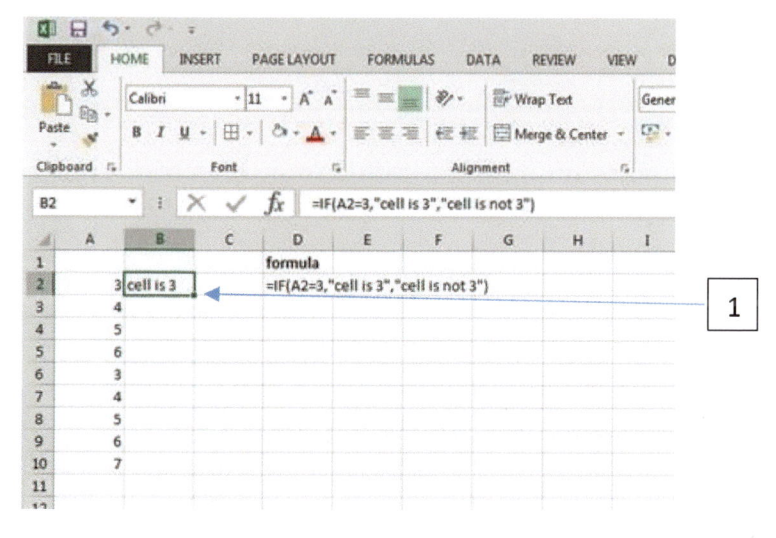

1) As can be seen, in the bottom right-hand corner of the cell, there is a pronounced square.
    a. Use the mouse and left-click on this square. Do not unclick the mouse yet
    b. Drag this square downwards, so you cover cells B2 to B10.

Figure 3.7: Click and drag function in Excel (2)

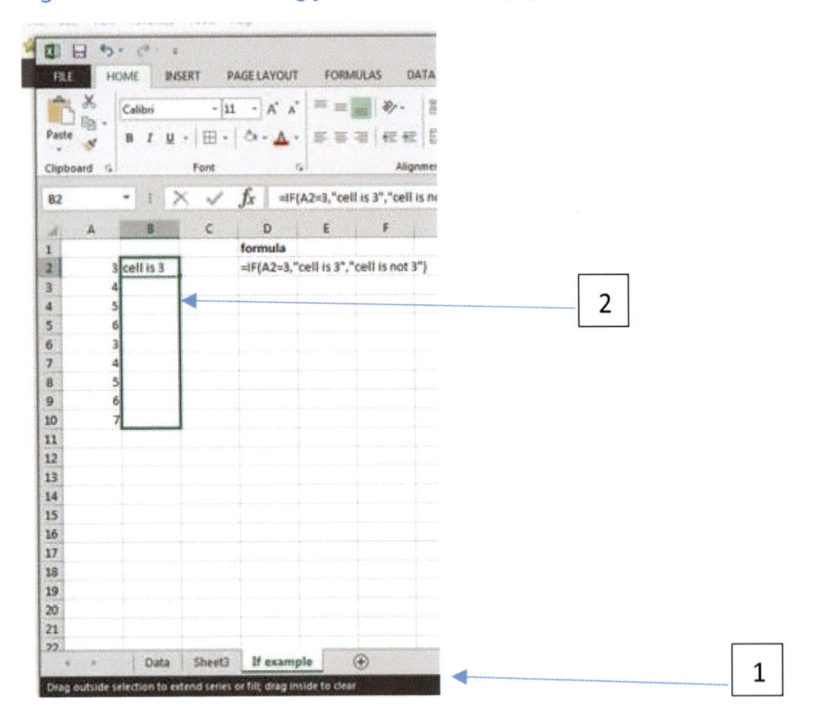

1) If you click on the bottom corner, you will see a message on the bottom of the Excel screen as shown
    a. This function can be used instead of copy and pasting, but be careful when using numbers, as Excel may use a cumulative counting process.
2) Now unclick the mouse to see the completed cells.

Figure 3.8: Click and drag function in Excel (3)

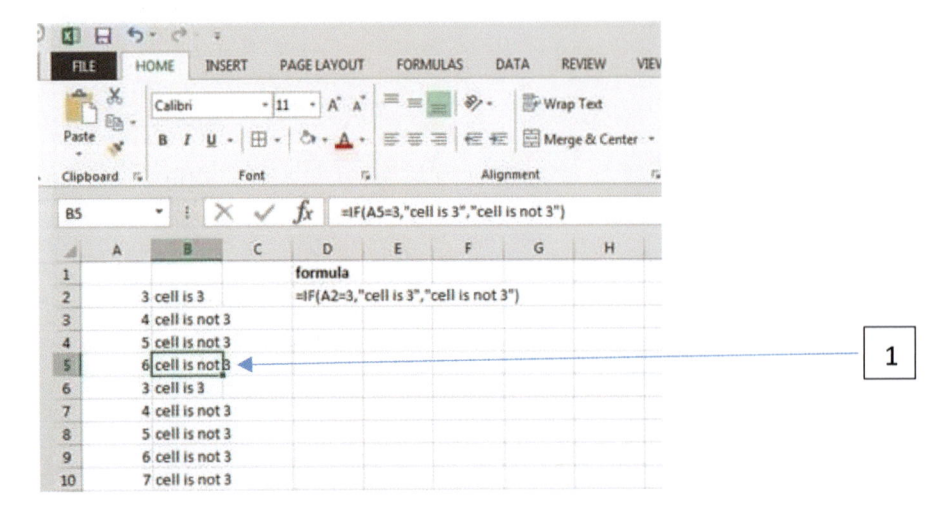

1) Click on any cell, and you will notice, that the formula has been updated to reflect the relevant cells… as demonstrated in figure 3.9.

Figure 3.9: Click and drag function in Excel – all of the if statements

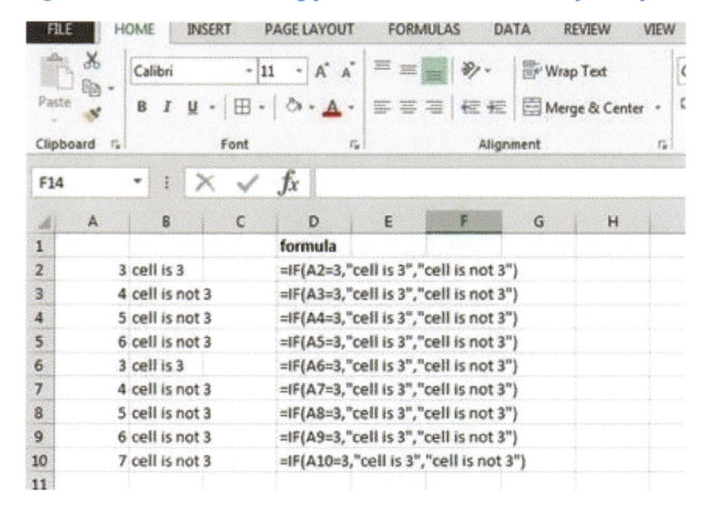

Not only does this drag function save valuable time, it can stop errors appearing from writing the formula (code) in different cells.

Back to binning the variables

As we have seen, the 'If' function is very powerful, but we have to create 4 bins, not 2.
The bins for income group are as follows:

- 5200 and under
- 5201 to 6000
- 6001 to 6800
- 6801 and above

The bins for the mortgage group are as follows:

- 31.7 and under
- 31.8 to 34.9
- 35.0 to 37.1
- 37.2 and above

Figure 3.10: Excel formula for income group:

=IF(C2<=5200,"5200 and under",IF(C2<=6000, "5201 to 6000", IF(C2<=6800,"6001 to 6800","6801 and above")))

Excel formula dissected:

- IF(C2<=5200,"5200 and under",
  - If income is less than or equal to 5200, then display "5200 and under"
- IF(C2<=6000, "5201 to 6000",
  - The value for under 5200 has been calculated previously
  - Else if income is less than or equal to 6000 then display "5201 to 6000",
    - This is the equivalent of greater than 5200 and less than or equal to 6000
- IF(C2<=6800,"6001 to 6800",
  - The value for under 6000 has been calculated previously
  - Else if income is less than or equal to 6800 then display "6001 to 6800",
    - This is the equivalent of greater than 6000 and less than or equal to 6800
- "6801 and above"
  - The values for under 6800 has been previously completed
- Finally, if all of the previous true_values are not found, then display "6801 and above.
- Always note the number of open brackets used, as the open and closed brackets need to balance

Excel reads the formula from left to right, therefore we have to be certain that it is written in the correct order. If we started the commands with 'C2<=6800', then proceeded with the 5200 and then the 6000, the 'if' formula would have failed. Using multiple 'if' statement can be confusing and you must keep count of the number of brackets used but, once completed it can make labelling cells very quick in Excel.

Figure 3.11: Excel formula for mortgage group

```
=IF(D2<=31.7,"31.7 and under", IF(D2<=34.9,"31.8 to 34.9",
IF(D2<=37.1,"35.0 to 37.1","37.2 and above")))
```

Excel formula dissected.

- IF(D2<=31.7,"31.7 and under",
  - If mortgage percent is equal to or less than 31.7 then display "31.7 and under"
- IF(D2<=34.9,"31.8 to 34.9",
  - Else if mortgage percent is equal to or less than 34.9 then display "31.8 to 34.9"
    - This is the equivalent of greater than 31.7 and less than or equal to 34.9

- IF(D2<=37.1,"35.0 to 37.1",
    - Else if mortgage percent is equal to or less than 37.1 then display "35.0 to 37.1"
        - This is the equivalent of greater than 31.7 and less than or equal to 37.1
- "37.2 and above"
    - Finally, if all of the previous true_values are not found, then display "37.2 and above."

Figure 3.12: Excel formula for mortgage group

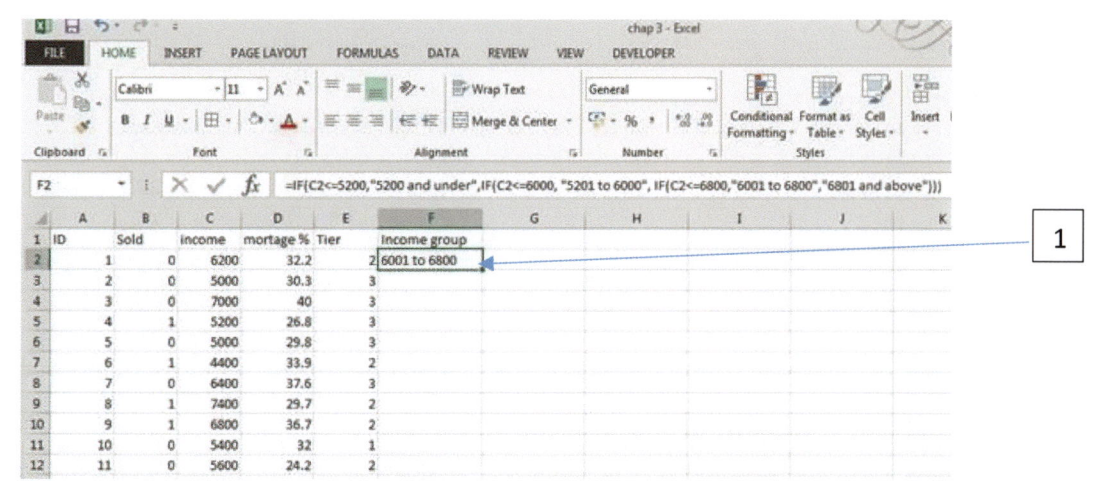

1) As before, as soon as you have completed the formula once,
    a. Click on the bottom right-hand corner of the cell and drag down, or
    b. double click on this square

Figure 3.13 contains a snapshot of the completed Excel sheet.

Figure 3.13: Completed Excel sheet

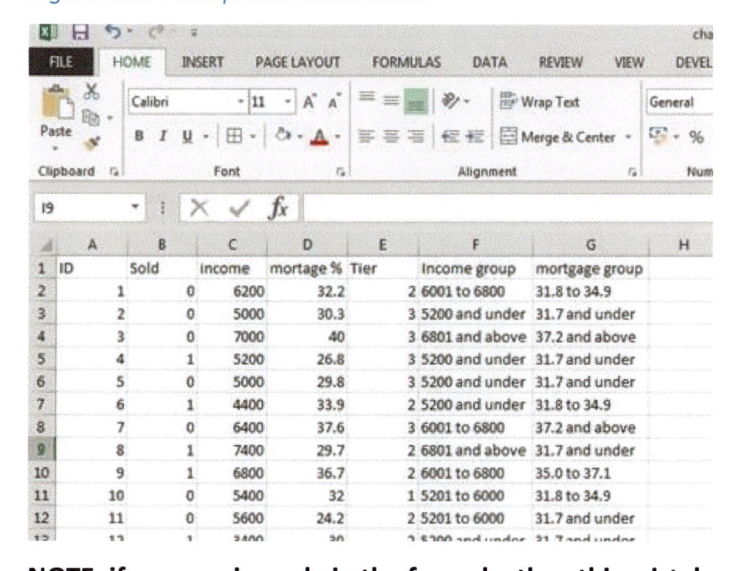

NOTE: if an error is made in the formula, then this mistake will be repeated in all of the other cells.

Always double check your work, e.g. ensure it displays 37.2 and not 3.72

3.3 Decision tree creation

We have now created a dataset (the Excel spreadsheet) that has the following columns
- id (customer id)
- sold (customer bought the product)
- income (income of customer)
- mortgage % (percentage of customers income is spent on the mortgage)
- tier (customer hierarchical)
- income group (income variable grouped)
- mortgage group (mortgage % variable grouped)

This dataset has 298 observations (rows) and 89 sales (targets).

For the first branch, we will be using chi-square statistics. As mentioned previously, chi-square tells us the probability of an event occurring by chance, using the observed and expected values. If we had a chi-square value of 0.01 this tells us that the observed results could have only happened by chance 1% of the times, therefore the lower the statistic, the better. As a basic rule of thumb, we want the chi-square statistic to be less than 0.05 (5%).

3.3.1 Pivot table

Our next step is to sum the total number of observations in each bin for the variables tier, income group and mortgage group individually. This can be easily calculated using pivot tables in Excel (which will be explored next), but our initial step requires us to add a new column to our dataset (Excel sheet) called count. This new column will contain the number 1 for all of the observations (rows).

Figure 3.14: Creating a new column

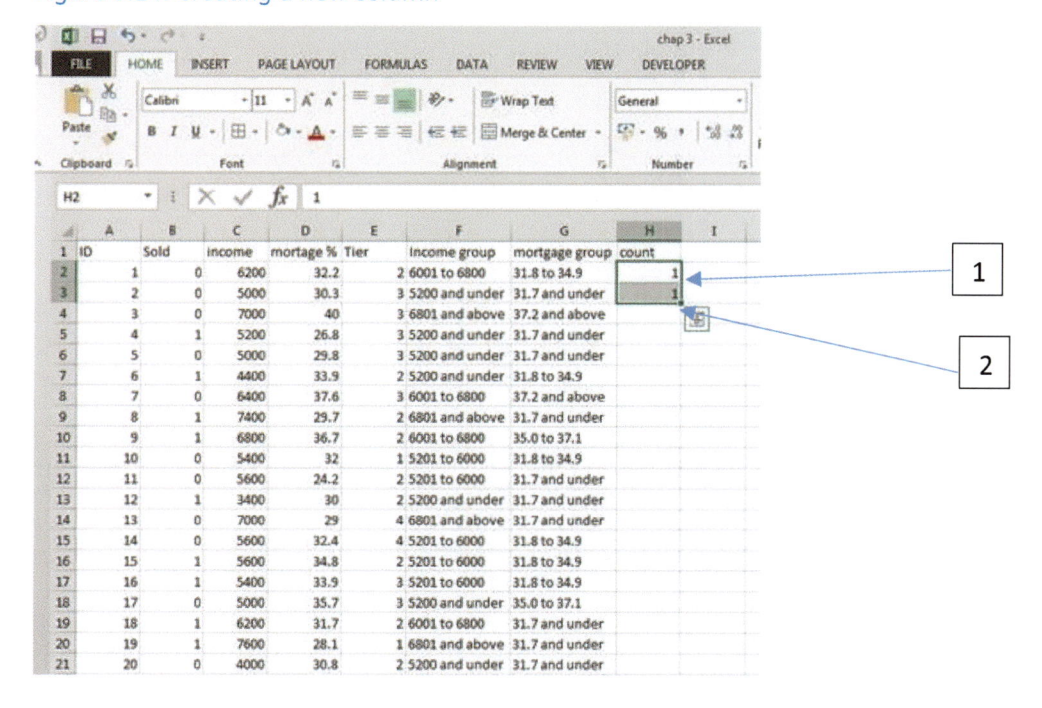

1) put the number 1 in the cells H2 and H3 (as shown above)
    a. highlight both cells with the mouse
2) As before, double-click the bottom right-hand corner of the highlighted cells to automatically fill the column.

Note: if you just put in 1 in just one of the cells and then double-click the cell, Excel will provide you with a cumulative count e.g. 1, 2, 3, 4, 5 … going all the way down to the bottom of the data, in this case, line 299

Figure 3.15: Excel new column completed

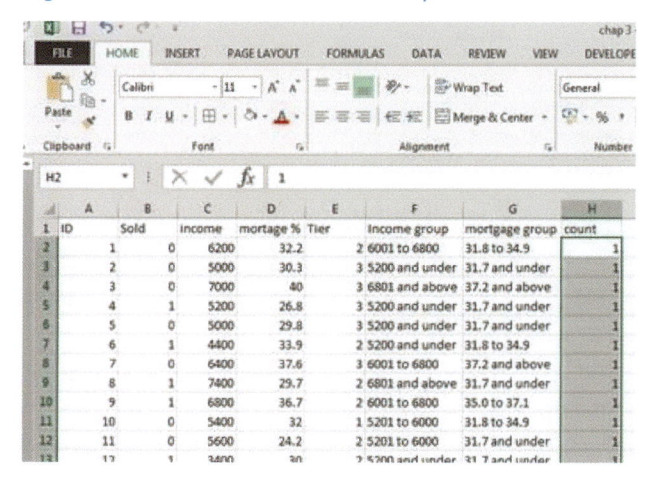

With the column completed, the next stage involves creating a pivot table.

Figure 3.16: Pivot table creation (1)

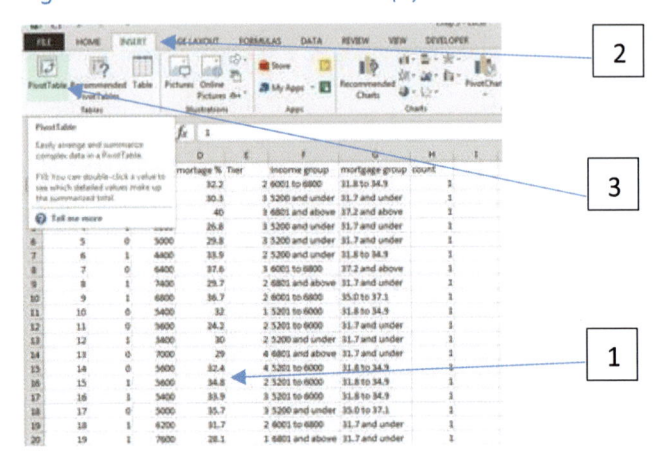

1) Click on a single cell within all the data
    a. do not highlight 2 or more cells as Excel will choose only use those cells highlighted to create the pivot table
2) Click on the **INSERT** tab on the top of the ribbon
3) Click on Pivot Table

Excel will automatically select the data you want

Figure 3.17: Pivot table creation (2)

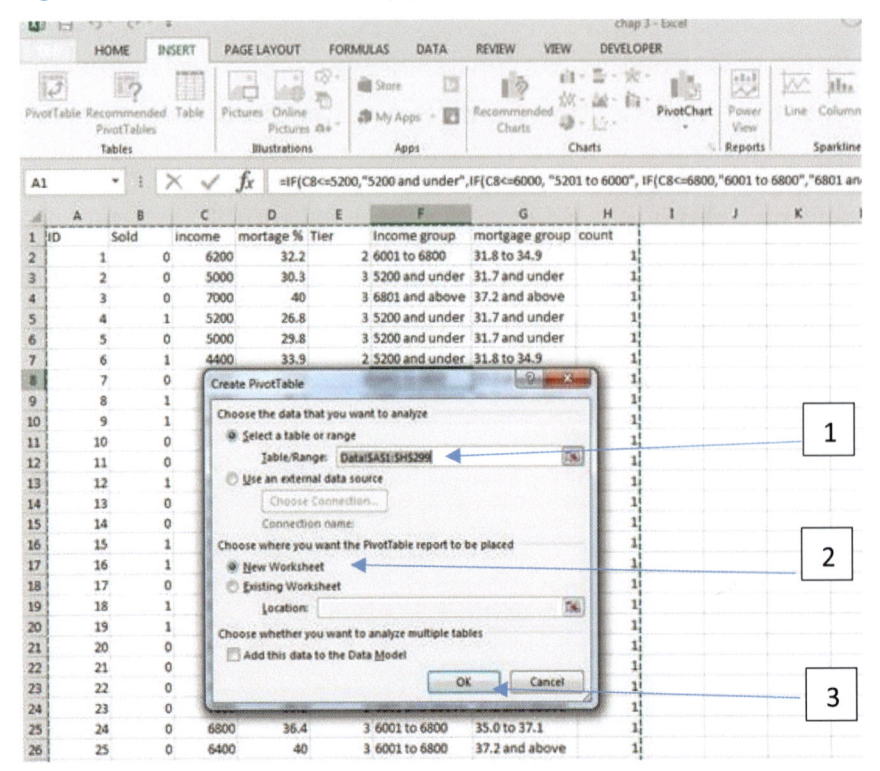

1) Data!$A$1:$H$299 - Excel has automatically completed this for you completed
    a. Data is the name of the sheet
    b. $A$1:$H$299, this tells Excel where the cells where the data is
2) Select New worksheet
3) Click OK

A new workbook will open for you, as demonstrated in figure 3.18.

Figure 3.18: Pivot table creation (3)

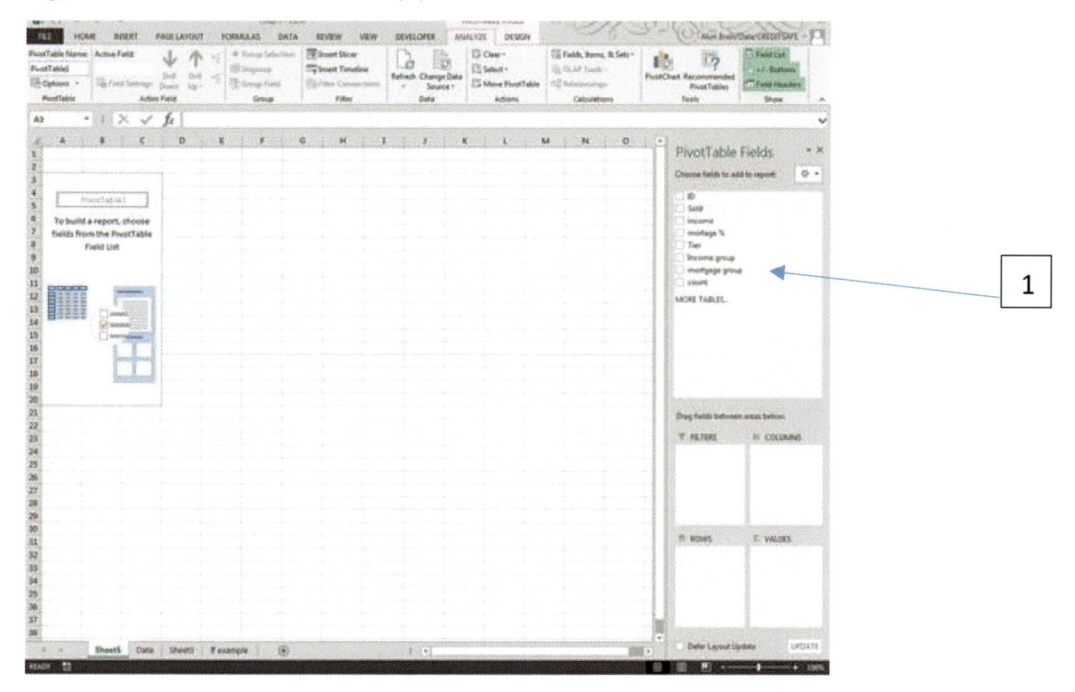

1) This list all of the columns available for the pivot table

The next step involves selecting the required data fields into the pivot table.

Figure 3.19: Pivot table selecting rows and values

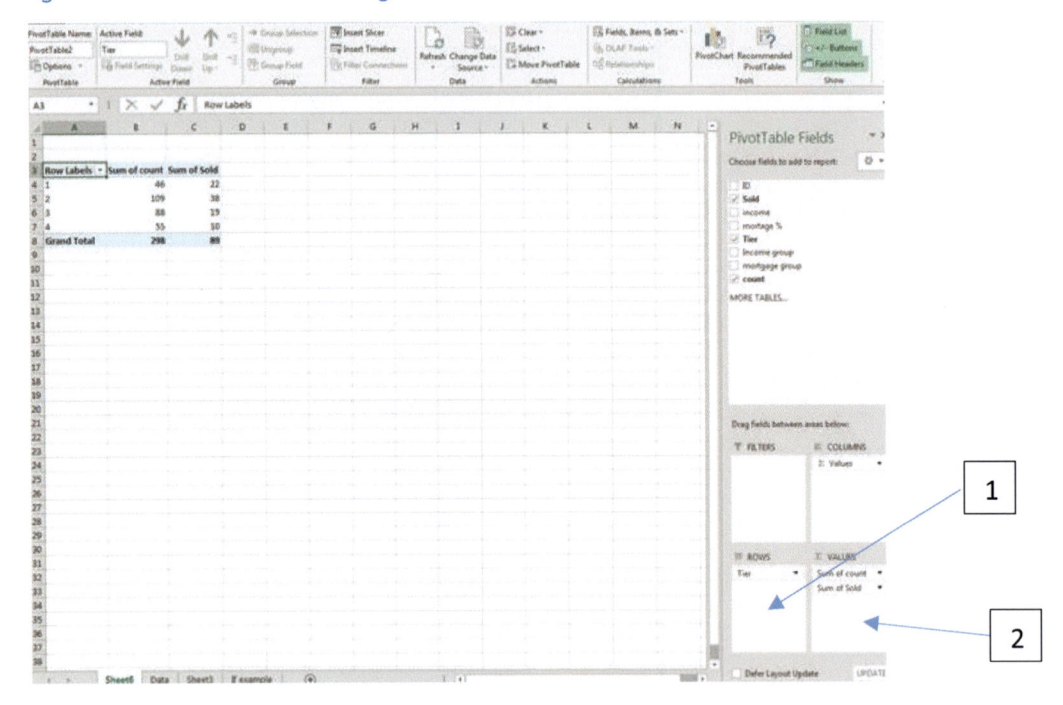

1) Click on **Tier** (do not unclick) and drag to the box called ROWS. Now unclick.
2) The variables we want to summarise are dragged in here.
    a. Click on **count** (do not unclick) and drag to the box called Values. Now unclick.
    b. Click on **Sold** (do not unclick) and drag to the box called Values. Now unclick.

Next stage requires us to calculate the percentage of sales, by inserting a calculated field.

Figure 3.20: Pivot table creating a calculated field (1)

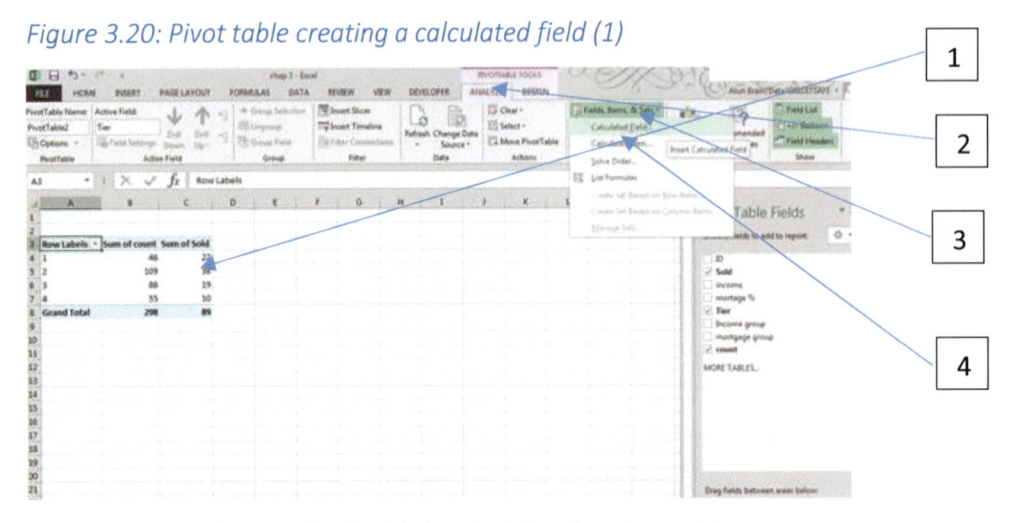

1) Ensure that a cell is highlighted within the pivot table
2) Click on the ANALYZE tab
3) Next click on Fields, Items & Sets
4) Select Calculated Field

Figure 3.21: Pivot table creating a calculated field (2)

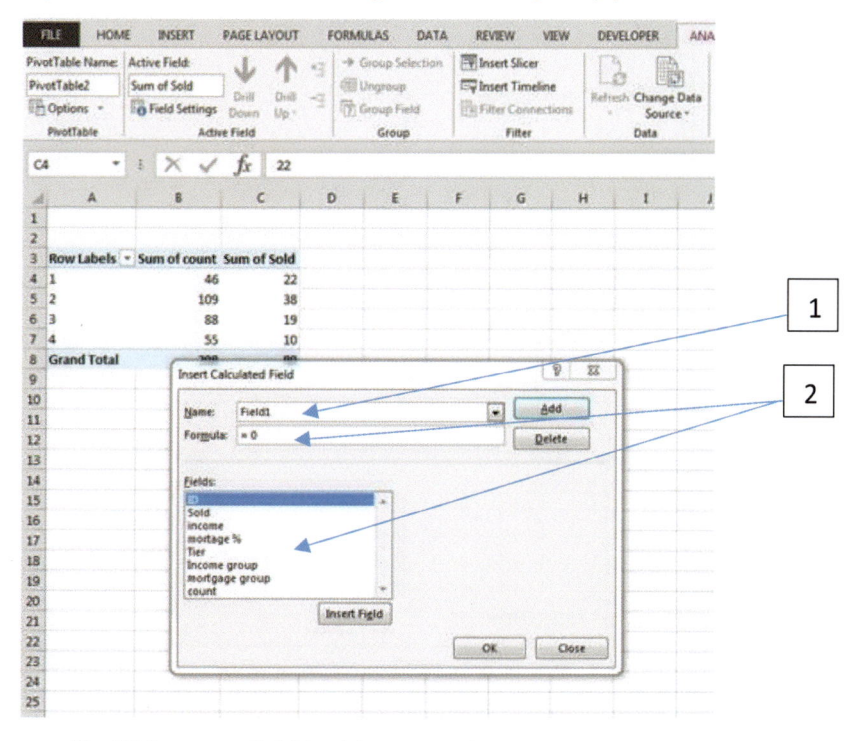

1) Write over Field1 with Perc_sale
2) In the Formula box, create the equation that will allow us to calculate the percentage of someone buying, sold / count
    a. Delete the 0 in the formula box (keep the =)
    b. Within the Fields box, double-click on **Sold**
    c. Now type **/**
    d. Next double click on **count**

Hopefully, the formula will resemble as displayed in figure 3.22

Figure 3.22: Pivot table creating a calculated field (3)

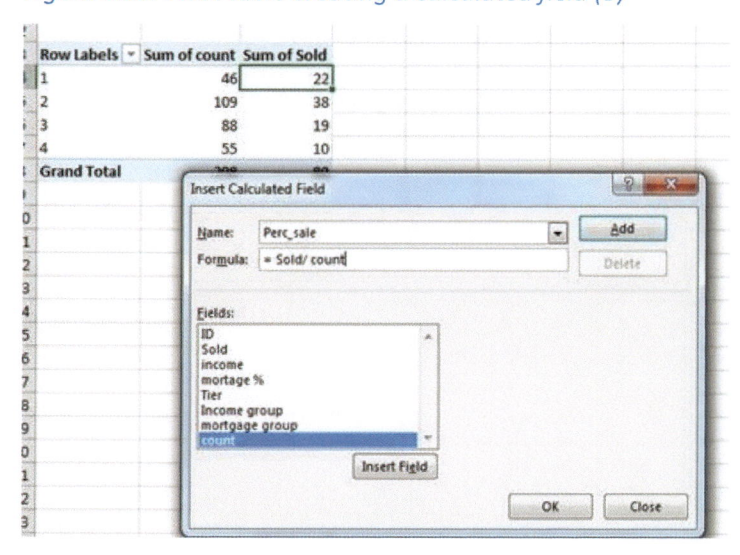

Now click OK

Figure 3.23: Pivot table creating a calculated field (4)

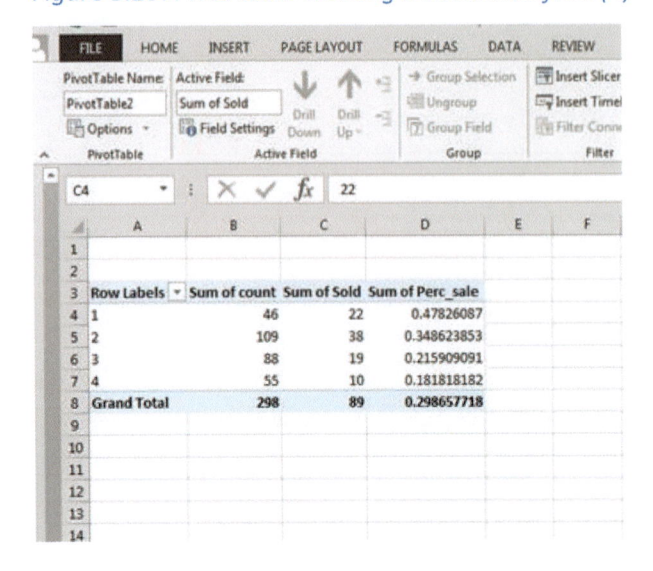

Next stage requires making the pivot Table more presentable

Figure 3.24: Formatting a pivot table (1)

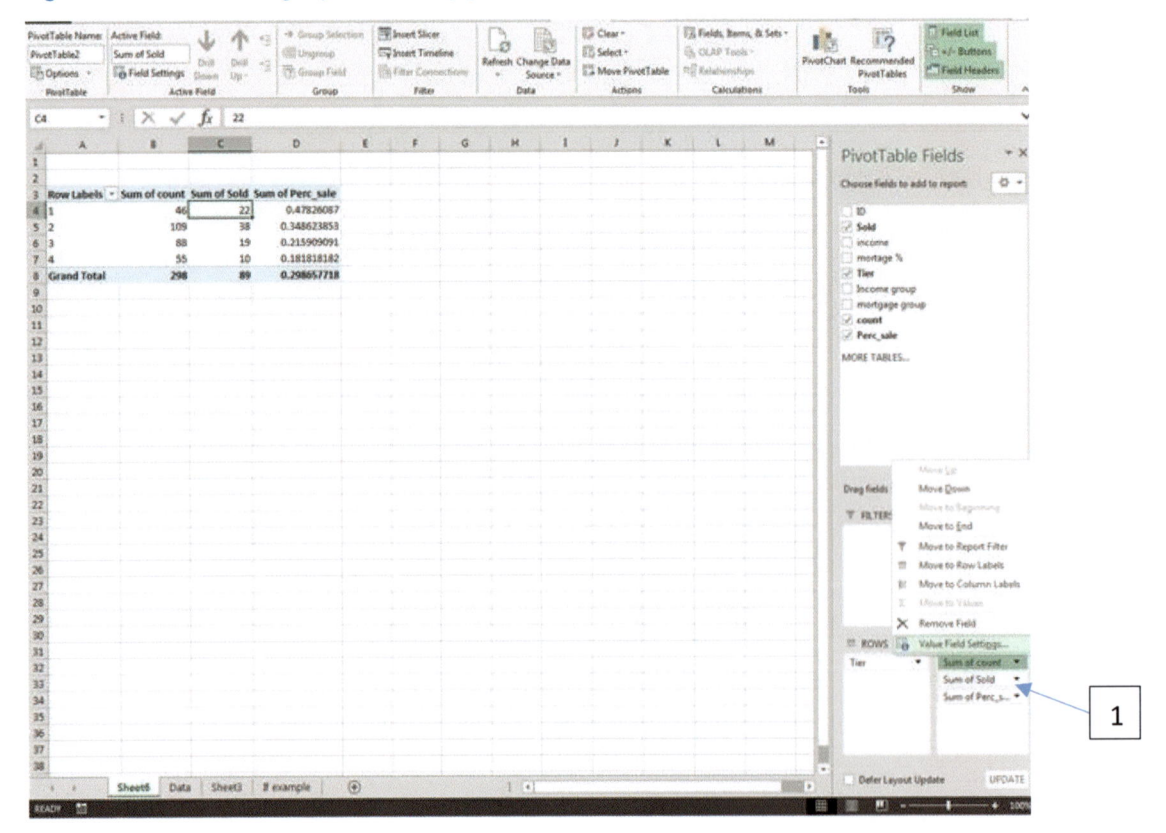

1) Click on Sum of count
    a. Select Value field settings

Figure 3.25: Formatting a pivot table (2)

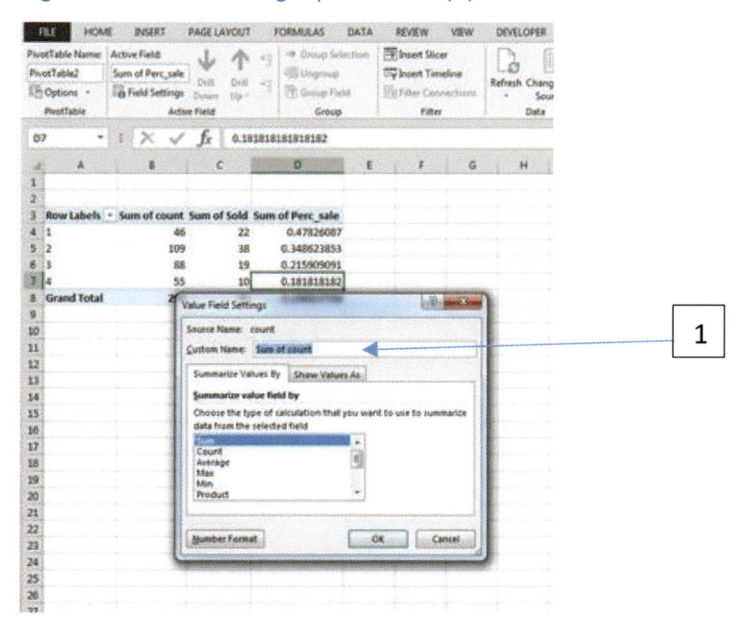

1) Change this to display Total as shown in figure 3.26

Figure 3.26: Formatting a pivot table (3)

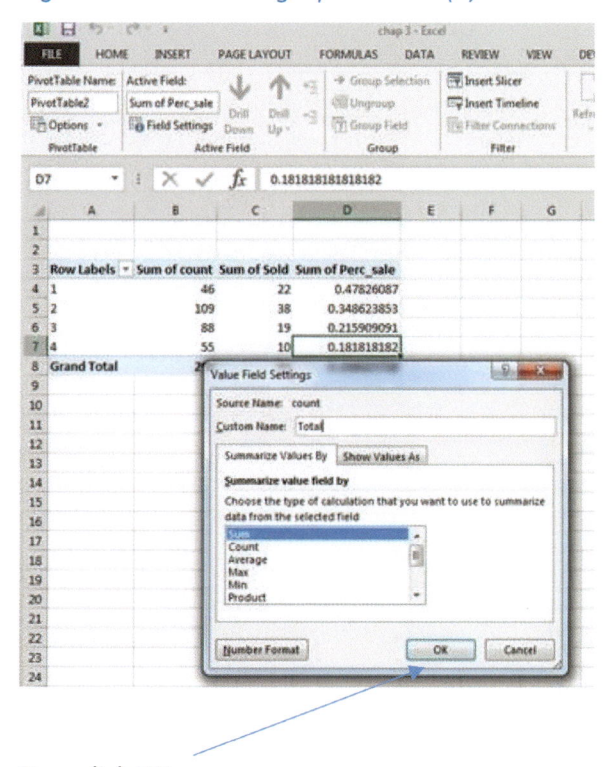

Now click OK

Figure 3.27: Formatting a pivot table (4)

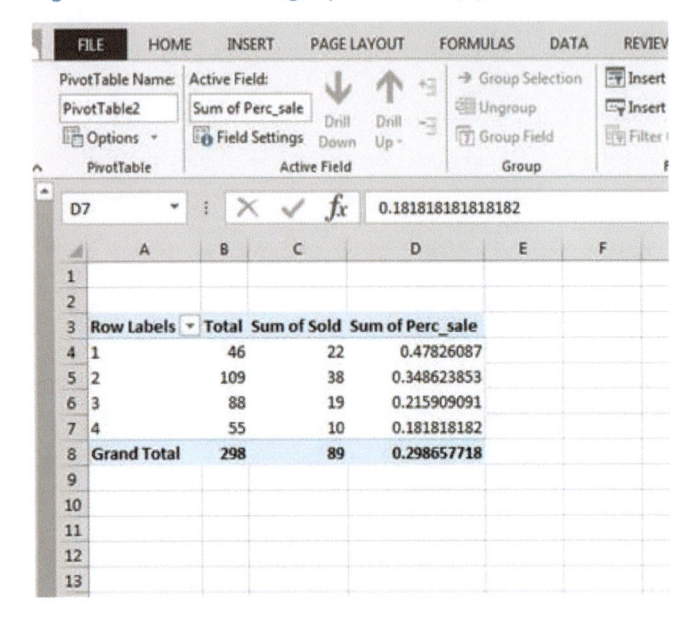

Repeat the same for Sold, but call this column Total Sold.

Figure 3.28: Formatting a pivot table (5)

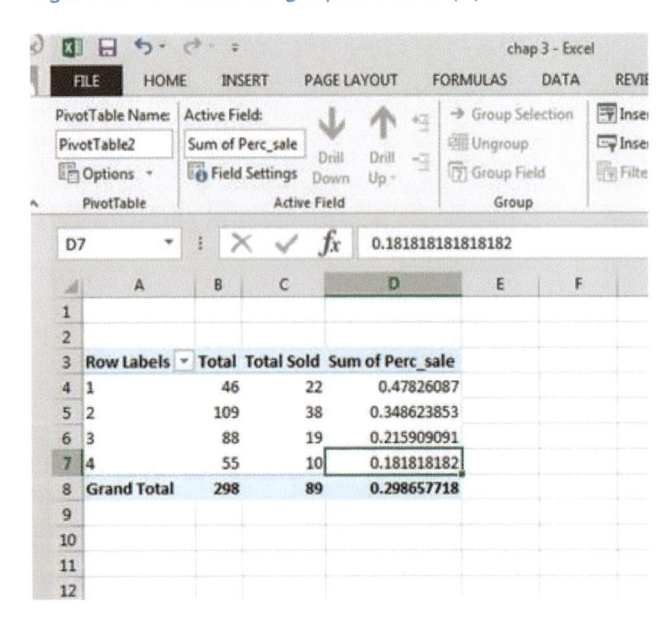

For 'Sum of Perc_sale', we want to change its name and make it display percentages (%).

Use the menu box 'Value Field Setting' for 'Sum of Perc_sale'.

Figure 3.29: Formatting a pivot table (5)

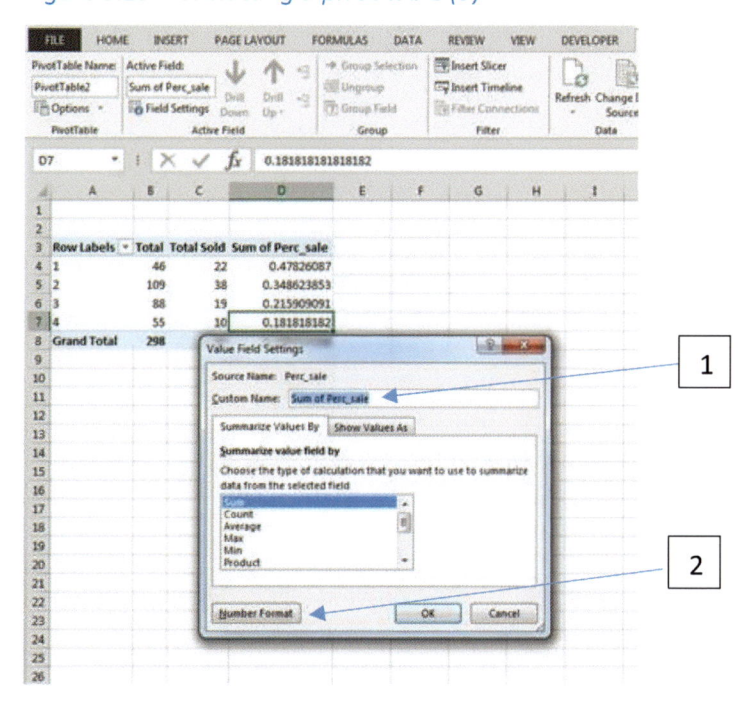

1) Change its name to % Sold
2) Click on Number Format

Figure 3.30: Formatting a pivot table (6)

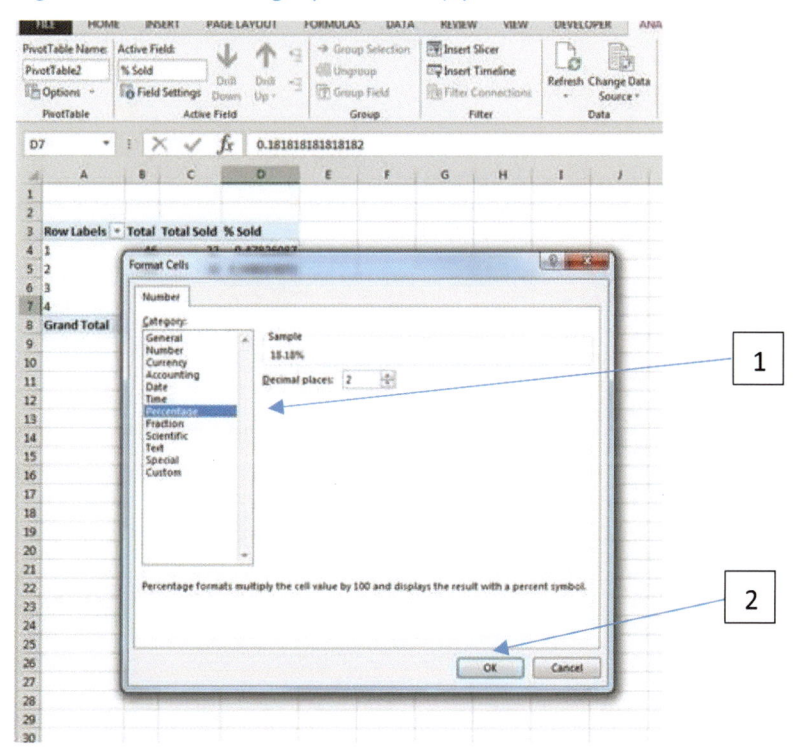

1) Select Percentage
2) Click OK

Then click OK on the 'Value Field Settings' box.

Figure 3.31: Formatting a pivot table - completed

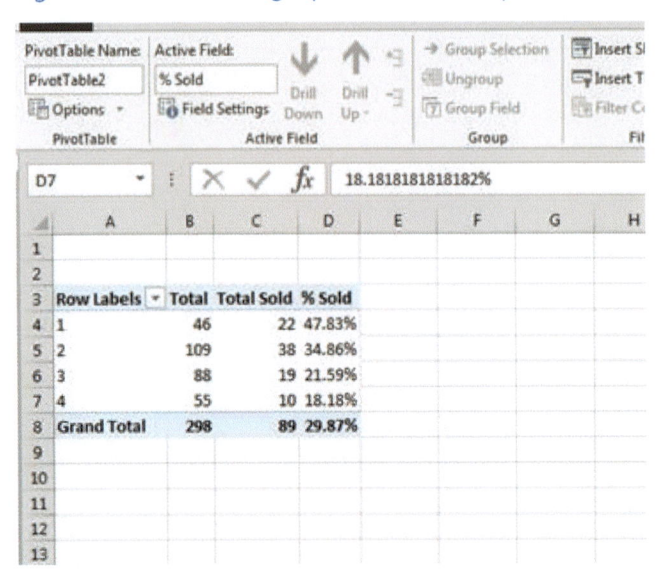

As you may recall, we need to compare the observed against the expected value. Overall, there is a 29.87% sales rate, so for each Tier calculate 29.87% of the total number of customers in each bin (the expected value).

This requires a new calculated field called 'Expected sales'.

- Ensure that a cell is highlighted within the pivot table
- Click on the ANALYZE tab
- Next click on Fields, Items & Sets
- Select Calculated Field

Figure 3.32: Creating expected sales column for chi-square

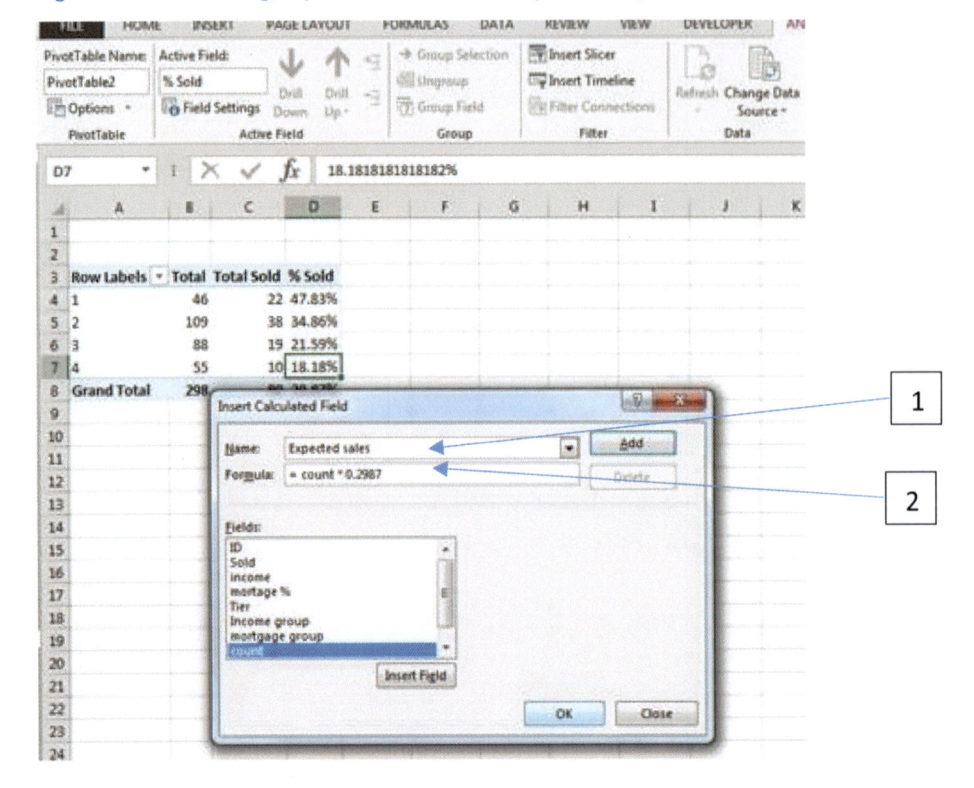

1) Name: Expected sales
2) Formula: = count * 0.2987

Excel does not like two columns labelled the same, and you may get an error message for 'Expected sales', in this case, just put a space before the 'E' in expected sales.

Figure 3.33: Result of expected sales column

Row Labels	Total	Total Sold	% Sold	Expected sales
1	46	22	47.83%	13.7402
2	109	38	34.86%	32.5583
3	88	19	21.59%	26.2856
4	55	10	18.18%	16.4285
Grand Total	298	89	29.87%	89.0126

With the expected and actual figures completed, we can calculate the chi-square statistics. Copy the formula as shown in figure 3.34, with a table detailing the results.

Figure 3.34: Chi-square result of tier

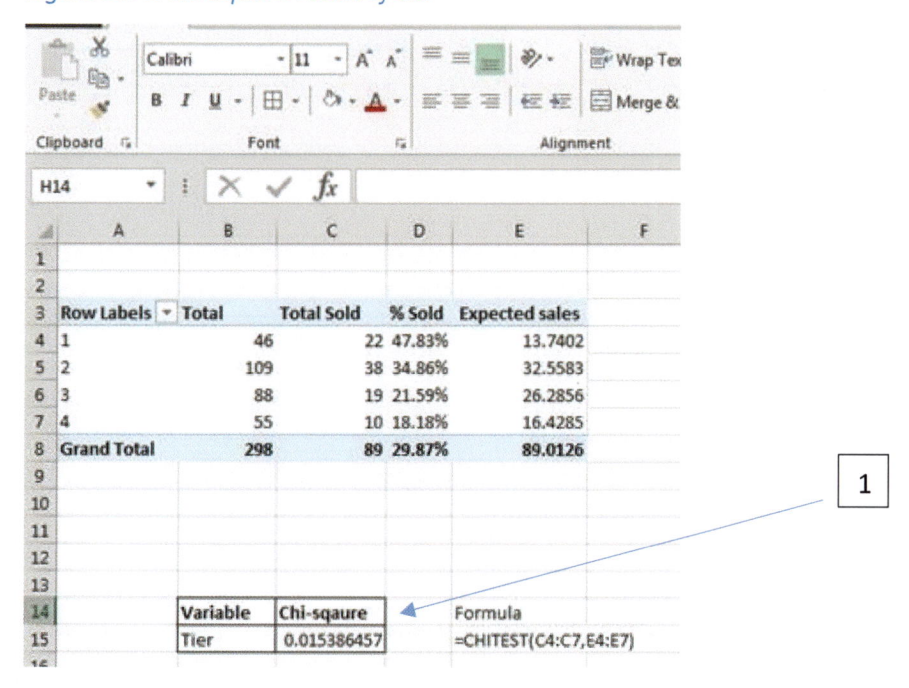

Row Labels	Total	Total Sold	% Sold	Expected sales
1	46	22	47.83%	13.7402
2	109	38	34.86%	32.5583
3	88	19	21.59%	26.2856
4	55	10	18.18%	16.4285
Grand Total	298	89	29.87%	89.0126

Variable	Chi-sqaure	Formula
Tier	0.015386457	=CHITEST(C4:C7,E4:E7)

[1]

1) For the variable Tier, we notice that the chi-square value is 0.015386, 1.5386% (this is low). To calculate the chi-square for Income group, as we have done the hard work already, it is easy.

Figure 3.35: Calculating the chi-square for income

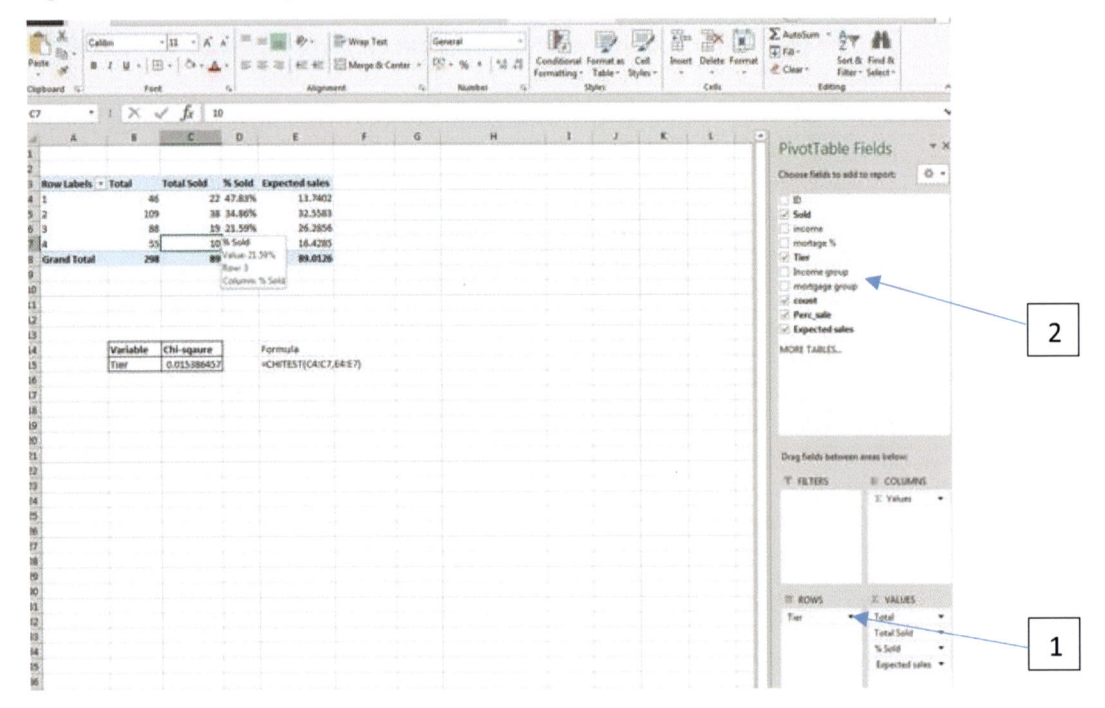

1) Click on Tier in the Rows Box (do not unclick)
    a. Drag it to the top box (unclick)
2) Click on Income group (do not unclick)
    a. Drag it to the Rows box (unclick)

Figure 3.36: Chi-square for income

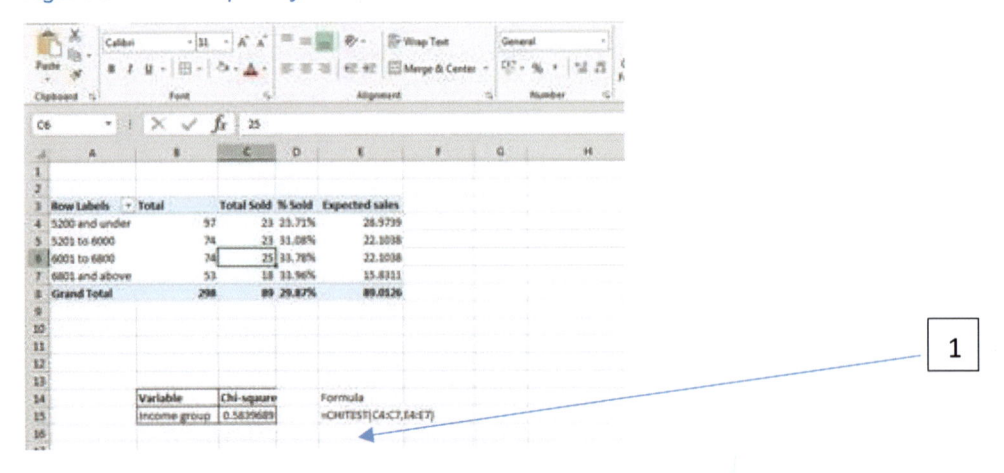

1) Ensure that the correct cells are being used to calculate the Chi-square statistic

For income group, Chi-square value is 0.583968, or 58.397% (this is very high)

Repeat the same for mortgage group

Figure 3.37: Chi-square for mortgage

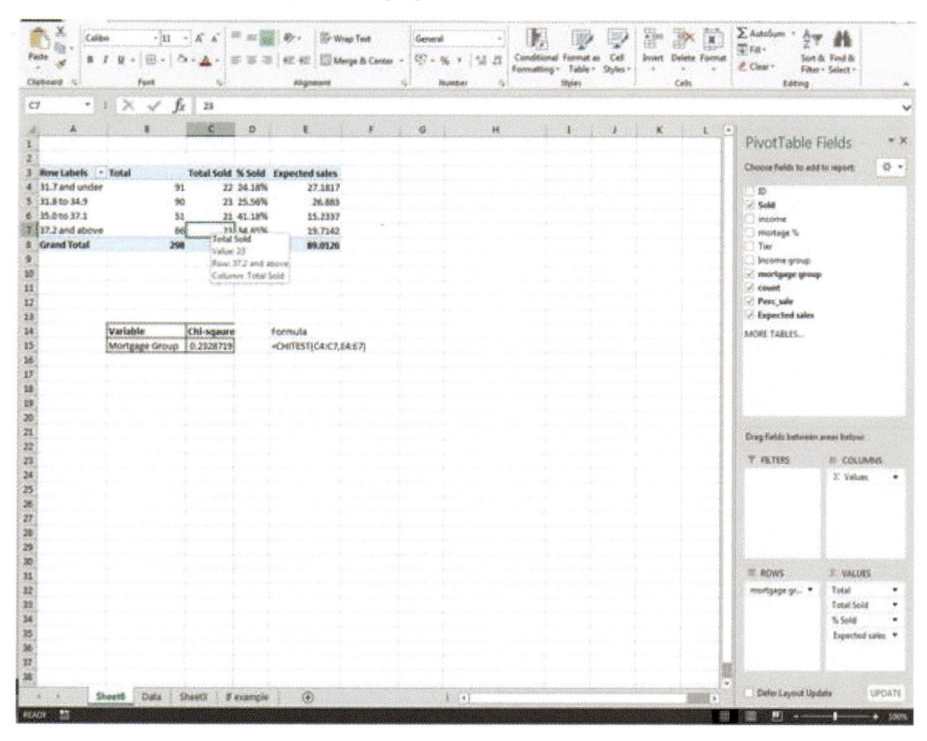

For mortgage group Chi-square value is 0.23237, or 23.237% (this is high).

Chi-square results are displayed in table 3.1

Table 3.1: Chi-square results

Variable	Chi-square
Tier	1.54%
Income Group	58.40%
Mortgage Group	23.24%

Based on the Chi-square results, the first branch will be created using the variable Tier, as it has the lowest chi-square statistic, and satisfies the under 5% rule. If no values satisfied the 5% rule, we would consider whether it would be wise to build a decision tree.

3.3.2 Designing a decision tree in Excel

Our first branch will contain the following figures

Table 3.2: Tier statistics results

Tier	Total	Total Sold	Not sold
1	46	22	24
2	109	38	71
3	88	19	69
4	55	10	45
Grand Total	**298**	**89**	**209**

Total and total sold were gathered from the Pivot table. 'Not sold' is calculated as follows

$$Not\ Sold = total - total\ sold$$

Figure 3.38: Initial decision tree

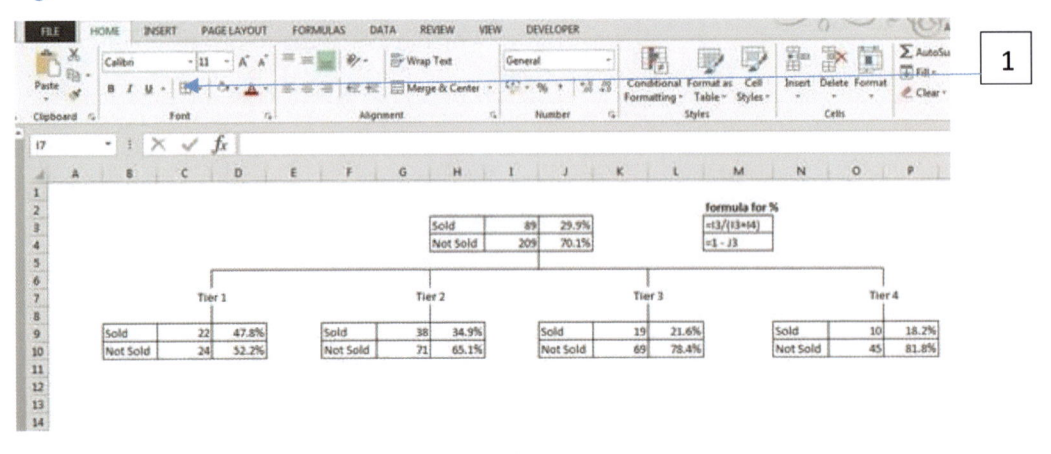

1) Using the Border button, we can simply create the decision tree, based on the most powerful variable (tier)

Figure 3.38, although insightful, can be considered quite boring. Adding some colour to the tree, with conditional formatting, creates a more eye-capturing tree.

Figure 3.39: Conditional formatting for decision tree creation

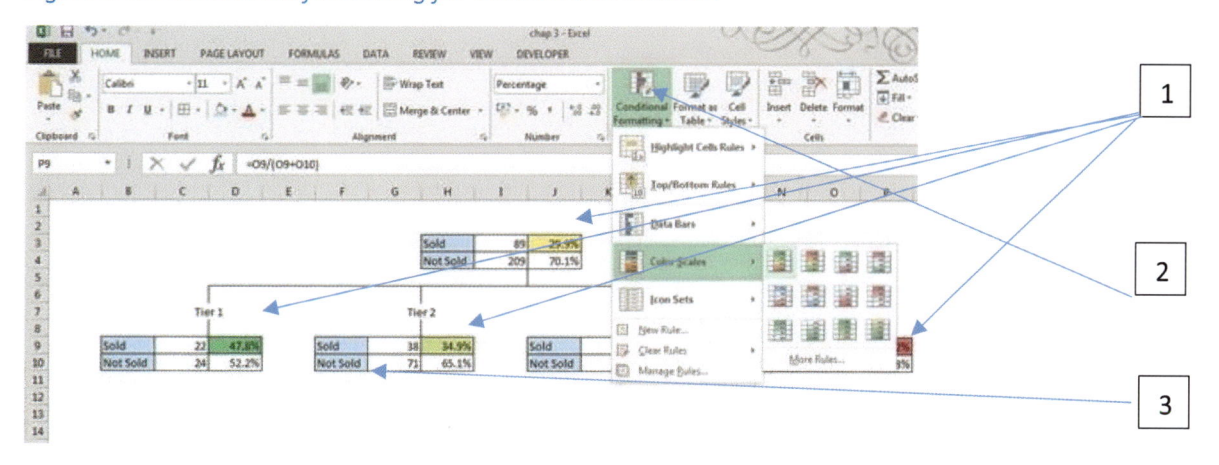

1) Using the CTRL and clicking on the cells, you can highlight all the cells you want to add conditional formatting to
    a. In this scenario Sold % cells have been highlighted
2) Select Colour scales and the second chart on the top row
3) Slightly colour these cells
    a. The labels sold and not sold have been coloured light blue

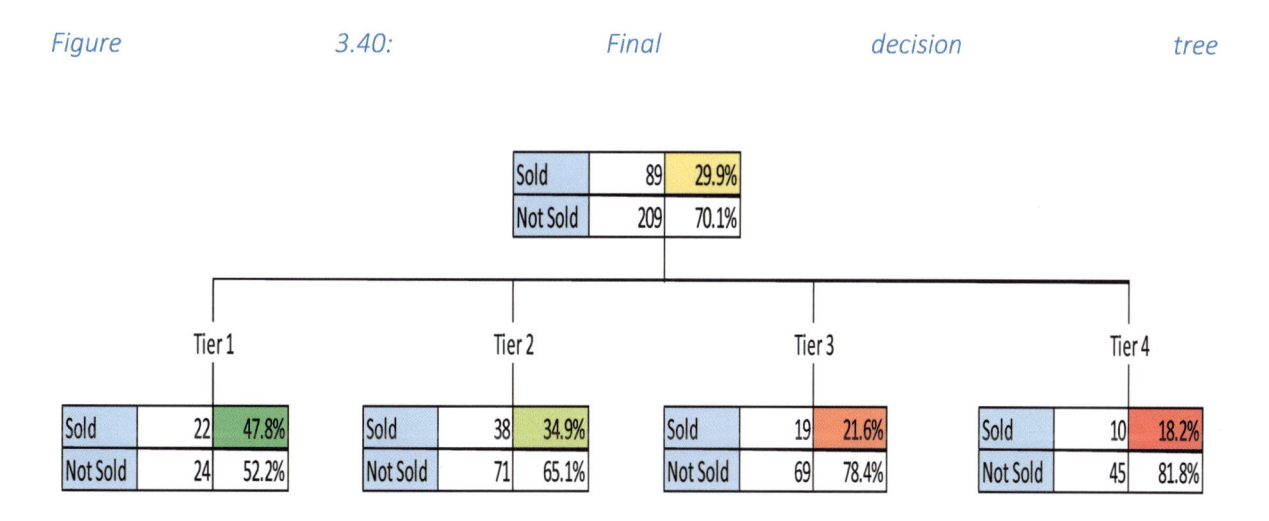

Figure   3.40:   Final   decision   tree

Back to the original question, is there a population that we can target cost effectively?

Using the decision tree, we would recommend targeting those customers in tier 1 and 2. Tier 1 is more than two and a half times more to buy than Tier 4!

This work could be considered extensive, but it was needed to discover the variable that discriminated against a product being sold or not the strongest. This will enable us to maximise our profits by targeting cost-effective customers.

3.7 Summary

Chapters 1 to 3 has shown us how powerful Excel can be for analysis. Additionally, it is a great education tool to explain statistics, simplistically. Excel can produce insightful graphs and is one of the most popular analytical tools in the workplace.

Sometimes we may have complex problems to solve that falls out of Excel remit. This is why we have specialised software to deal with complex problems. The next stage of this book uses Python to further enhance our statistical knowledge.

4 Introduction to Python

Python is a free and open source data analytical tool that allows you to interrogate large datasets and conduct complex analysis. Python is a scripting language, which means that you have to write the code (which we introduced slightly in Excel with 'IF' statements).
This book uses Spyder, from https://www.anaconda.com/

This chapter covers the very basics of statistics within Python), so as to remove any presumption of previous capabilities

Python does not have all of the tools you need when you initially install it, therefore as you progress with Python, you will not download these tools (packages/libraries). Packages are collections of Python functions, which can be used once installed.
The aims of this chapter is:
- Understand how to use different data types
    - Lists
    - Arrays
    - Data frames
- Calculate simple statistics (mean, mode, chi-square etc...)
- Create basic graphs

4.1 Spyder

With plenty of advice and videos on the internet detailing how to download and install Python, this book will start at the opening screen for Spyder. I have a preference for consoles, whereas other prefer Jupyter notebook. The code will work in any environment.

Figure 4.1: Spyder

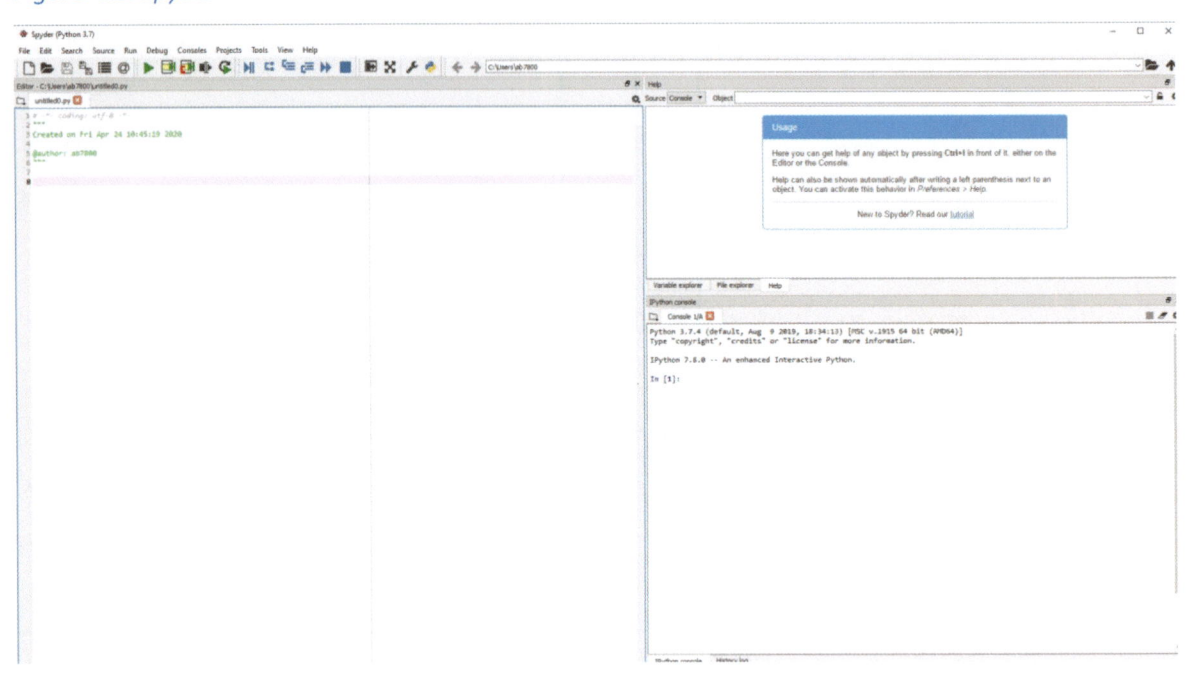

This book replicates certain sections from chapters 1 to 3 as a way to demonstrate how to program in Python. This will also provide a platform on how to transfer Excel knowledge to Python and to check our results. Unlike Excel where progress is easily observable, Python does not display the results to you as soon as you write your code.

Rather than explain the different segments in Python, this book will guide you using examples.

Through years of experience, I have discovered that 'doing it' is more productive than long introductions. Therefore, this chapter is an applied approach to learning the basics in Python.

The two most important libraries to use in this book are

Program 4-1: Initial libraries

```
import numpy as np
import pandas as pd
```

As a quick way to run code, highlight the code with your mouse, then press **Shift** and **Enter**.

This will run your code. Running these two libraries will not create any magnificent outcome, but will equip you for the following exercises

Figure 4.2: Activating libraries

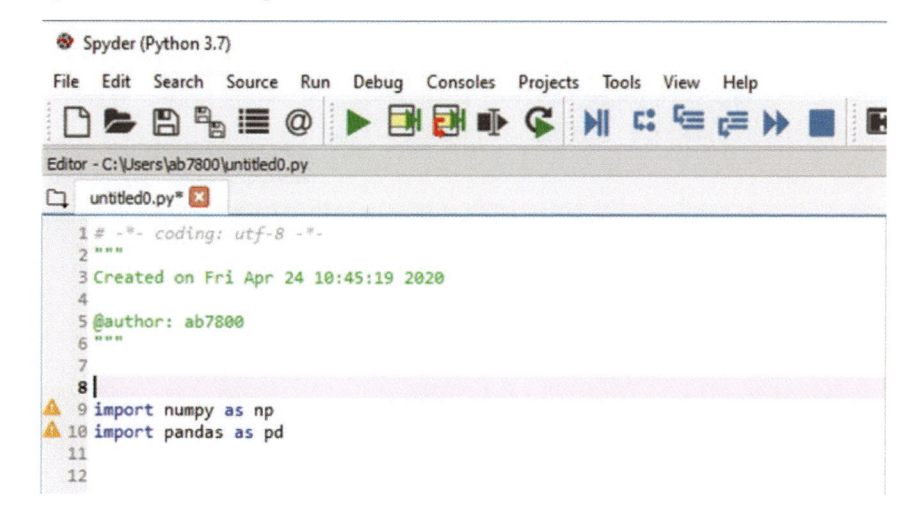

Ignore the exclamation marks in triangles, this just tells us that we have not written any code that uses these libraries.

4.2 Excel to Python

Our first example is to replicate 'Example 1.2.1', calculating the mean, median and range, but in Python.

4.2.1 Example of mean, median and range

Use Python to calculate the average (mean), median, mode, and range for the following list of values:

13, 18, 13, 14, 13, 16, 14, 21, 13

To complete this task, we first need to create a list.

Program 4-2: Creating a list of numbers

```
a = [13, 18, 13, 14, 13, 16, 14, 21, 13]
```

If you run the code above (**shift** and **enter**), then you will create the list of numbers, with a variable called **a.** Figures 4.3 to 4.5 displays snapshots of the 3 different screens in Spyder.

Figure 4.3: Code section

[Screenshot of Spyder IDE showing code with callout "Our list code" pointing to `a = [13, 18, 13, 14, 13, 16, 14, 21, 13]`]

The code that has been run.

Figure 4.4: Variable explorer

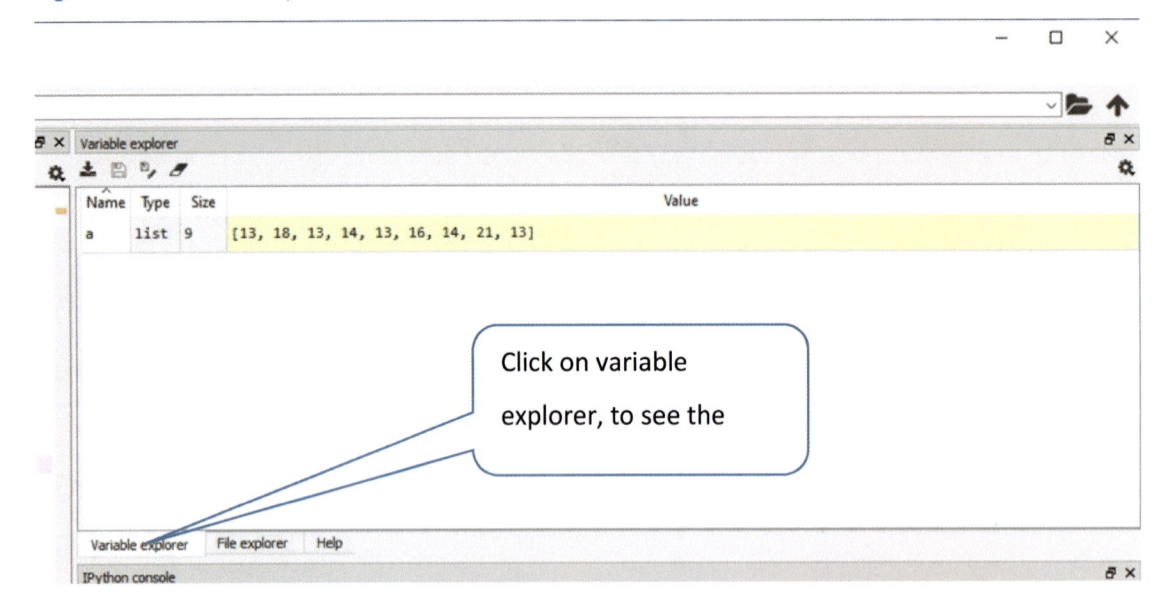

[Screenshot of Variable explorer showing variable `a`, type list, size 9, value [13, 18, 13, 14, 13, 16, 14, 21, 13], with callout "Click on variable explorer, to see the"]

Displays our list, with the information.

Figure 4.5: Console section

[Screenshot of IPython console showing:
Python 3.7.4 (default, Aug 9 2019, 18:34:13) [MSC v.1915 64 bit (AMD64)]
Type "copyright", "credits" or "license" for more information.

IPython 7.8.0 -- An enhanced Interactive Python.

In [1]: import numpy as np
   ...: import pandas as pd
   ...:
   ...:
   ...: a = [13, 18, 13, 14, 13, 16, 14, 21, 13]

In [2]:

with callout "To show that code has run succesfully"]

Next stage involves calculating the mean, median and mode of the variable **a**.

Program 4-3: Calculating the mean

```
np.mean(a)
```

The **np**, signifies that we need to use the library numpy, to calculate the mean.

The second part, **mean(a),** tells Python that we want the mean of the variable **a**.

You must remember the brackets or you will get an error message.

Figure 4.6: First error in Python

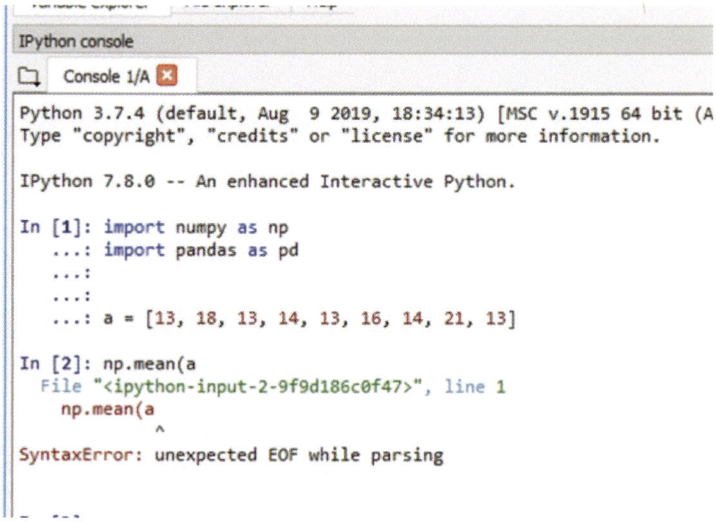

```
IPython console
Console 1/A
Python 3.7.4 (default, Aug  9 2019, 18:34:13) [MSC v.1915 64 bit (A
Type "copyright", "credits" or "license" for more information.

IPython 7.8.0 -- An enhanced Interactive Python.

In [1]: import numpy as np
   ...: import pandas as pd
   ...:
   ...:
   ...: a = [13, 18, 13, 14, 13, 16, 14, 21, 13]

In [2]: np.mean(a
  File "<ipython-input-2-9f9d186c0f47>", line 1
    np.mean(a
            ^
SyntaxError: unexpected EOF while parsing
```

Error messages are nothing to be scared of, and can sometimes help. If everyone was perfect at Python, then there would be no need for error messages. In figure 4.6 an error has been produced as an example.

Correcting the code and using brackets

Figure 4.7: Calculating the mean in Python

```
SyntaxError: unexpected EOF while parsing


In [3]:

In [3]: np.mean(a)
Out[3]: 15.0

In [4]:
```

Using the console section, we can view the code that has been run, along with the result, **15.0,** which matches our Excel result. In Excel, we used the command average, the same as in Python.

Median will be calculated next (as numpy does not calculate mode). As you can see in program 4-4, the code is very similar to calculating the mean.

Program 4-4: Calculating the median

```
np.median(a)
```

Figure 4.8: Results from calculating the median

```
In [5]:

In [5]: np.median(a)
Out[5]: 14.0

In [6]:
```

The median is shown as 14.

Finally, we will calculate the range. In section 1.3 we had shown the Excel command as

```
=MAX (range) - MIN (range)
```

We amend this slightly and write it in Python

Program 4-5: Calculating the range in Python

```
np.max(a) - np.min(a)
```

Again, highlight the code and run it.

Figure 4.9: Results from calculating the range

```
In [4]: np.mean(a)
Out[4]: 15.0

In [5]: np.median(a)
Out[5]: 14.0

In [6]: np.max(a) - np.min(a)
Out[6]: 8
```

The next stage involves calculating the mode, standard deviation and variance. This involves using a new library, **statistics.**

Program 4-6: Calculating further statistics

```
import statistics
from statistics import variance
from statistics import mode
from statistics import stdev


variance(a)
mode(a)
stdev(a)
```

Figure 4.10: Results from calculating further statistics

```
In [6]: np.max(a) - np.min(a)
Out[6]: 8

In [7]: import statistics
   ...: from statistics import variance
   ...: from statistics import mode
   ...: from statistics import stdev

In [8]: variance(a)
Out[8]: 8

In [9]: mode(a)
Out[9]: 13

In [10]: stdev(a)
Out[10]: 2.8284271247461903

In [11]:
```

Figure 4.11: Results from figure 1.5

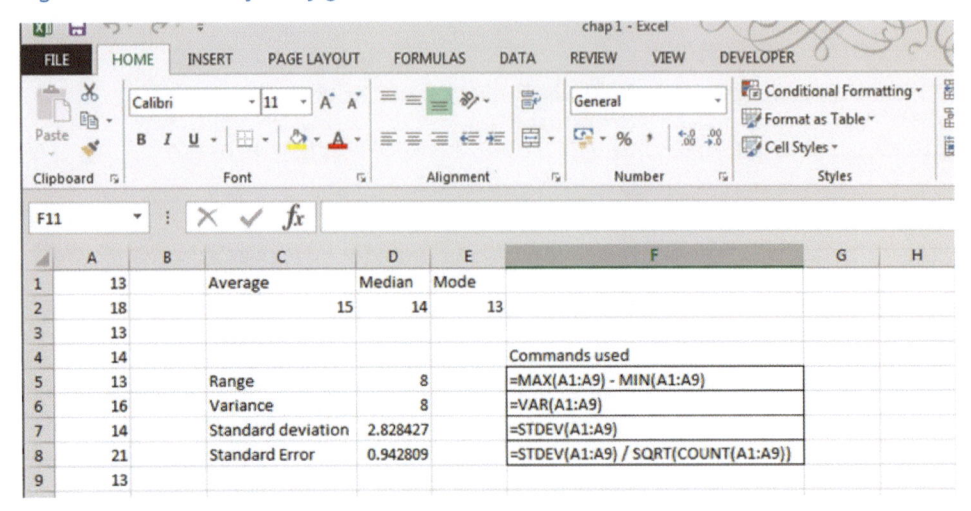

We have now recreated our Excel statistics in Python.

The choice to use Python instead of Excel for basic statistics is mainly personal, this book is designed just to provide the foundations of applied statistics.

4.3 Correlation

Next task is to recreate the correlation statistics and graphs in Python from figure 1.11.   (This uses program 2 Correlation)

Figure 4.12: Copy of figure 1.11

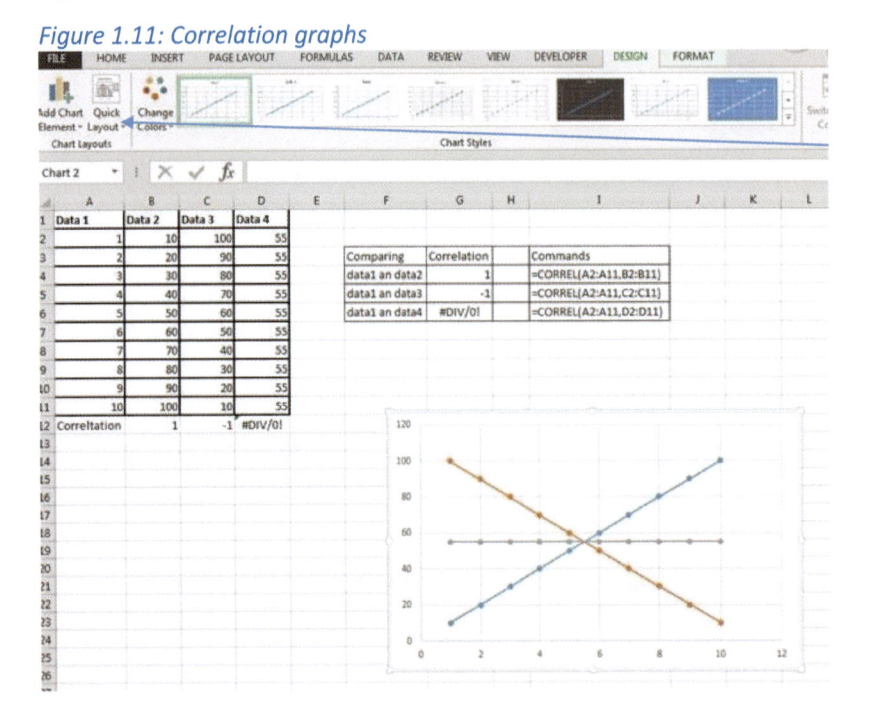

This will entail:

- creating 4 new lists
- carrying out correlation tests
- producing a graph

Our first step requires creating 4 new lists.

To mimic the Excel example, they will be called data1, data2, data3 and data4.

Program 4-7: Creating the correlation data

```
data1 = [1,2,3,4,5,6,7,8,9,10]
data2 = [10,20,30,40,50,60,70,80,90,100]
data3 = [100,90,80,70,60,50,40,30,20,10]
data4 = [55,55,55,55,55,55,55,55,55,55]
```

All four lines can be run at the same time, by highlighting them and pressing **shift** and **enter**.

The command to conduct the correlation test is **pearsonr()** *(this uses Pearson-test)*. This produces a **result** with two values:

- The correlation coefficient
- The p-value

The **p-value** is ustilised when you're testing a hypothesis. The p-value is an important measure, which has been discussed previously in this book.

Program 4-8: Calculating the correlation in Python

```
# import the library
from scipy.stats import pearsonr
# calculate Pearson's correlation
pearsonr(data1, data2)
pearsonr(data1, data3)
pearsonr(data1, data4)
```

Comparing our Excel code, to the Python code, we notice some similarity.

Table 4.1: Comparing Excel and Python code for correlation

Excel Formula	Python version
=CORREL(A2:A11,B2:B11)	pearsonr(data1, data2)
=CORREL(A2:A11,C2:C11)	pearsonr(data1, data3)
=CORREL(A2:A11,D2:D11)	pearsonr(data1, data4)

A2:A11 is the same as data1, B2:B11 is the same as data2 etc...

Figure 4.13: Python results for correlation

```
In [10]: data1 = [1,2,3,4,5,6,7,8,9,10]
    ...: data2 = [10,20,30,40,50,60,70,80,90,100]
    ...: data3 = [100,90,80,70,60,50,40,30,20,10]
    ...: data4 = [55,55,55,55,55,55,55,55,55,55]

In [11]: from scipy.stats import pearsonr

In [12]: pearsonr(data1, data2)
Out[12]: (1.0, 0.0)

In [13]: pearsonr(data1, data3)
Out[13]: (-1.0, 0.0)

In [14]: pearsonr(data1, data4)
C:\Users\ab7800\AppData\Local\Continuum\anaconda3\lib\site-packages\scipy\stats\stats.py:3399:
PearsonRConstantInputWarning: An input array is constant; the correlation coefficent is not defined.
  warnings.warn(PearsonRConstantInputWarning())
Out[14]: (nan, nan)

In [15]:
```

The results produced in Python are the same as those in Excel, with a warning for data1 and data4, as expected.

Table 4.2: Python Correlation results

Combination	Result
Data1 and data2	1
Data1 and data3	-1
Data1 and data4	Nan

The next part of this exercise requires building a graph. This requires further coding and rather than give the solution in one go, we will progress step-by-step.

First, we need a new library

Program 4-9: import the plotting library

```
# import the library
import matplotlib.pyplot as plt
```

Program 4-10: Plot one line

```
plt.plot(data1, data2, 'blue')
plt.show()
```

- **plt.plot** - the command to produce our plot
- **(data1, data2, 'blue')**
    - **Data1** – the x –axis
    - **Data2** - the y-axis
    - **'blue'** – tells python that the line is blue
- **Plt.show()** – the command to tell Python to plot the chart

Figure 4.14: Initial plot

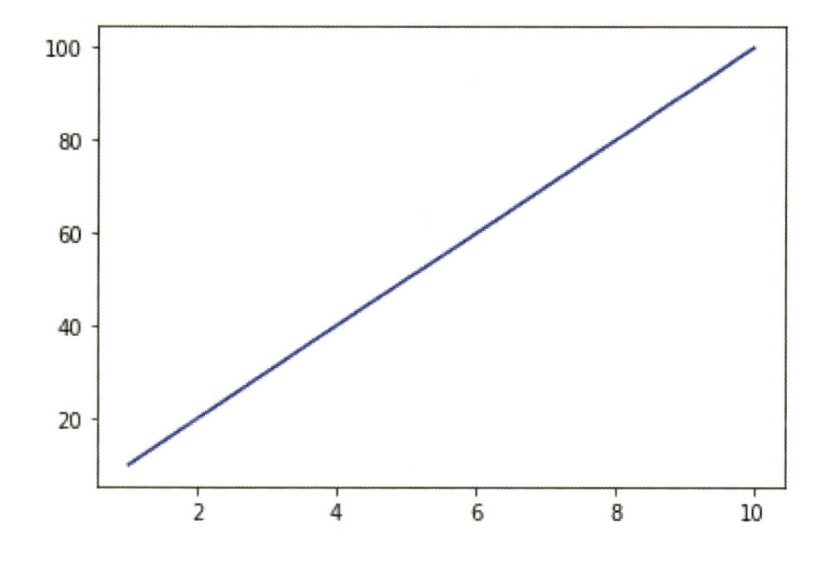

To add on further data onto the same chart is straight forward

Program 4-11: Plot all lines

```
plt.plot(data1, data2, 'blue')
plt.plot(data1, data3, 'orange')
plt.plot(data1, data4, 'grey')

plt.show()
```

You must run all of this code at the same time, or it won't work

Figure 4.15: Final Correlation plot

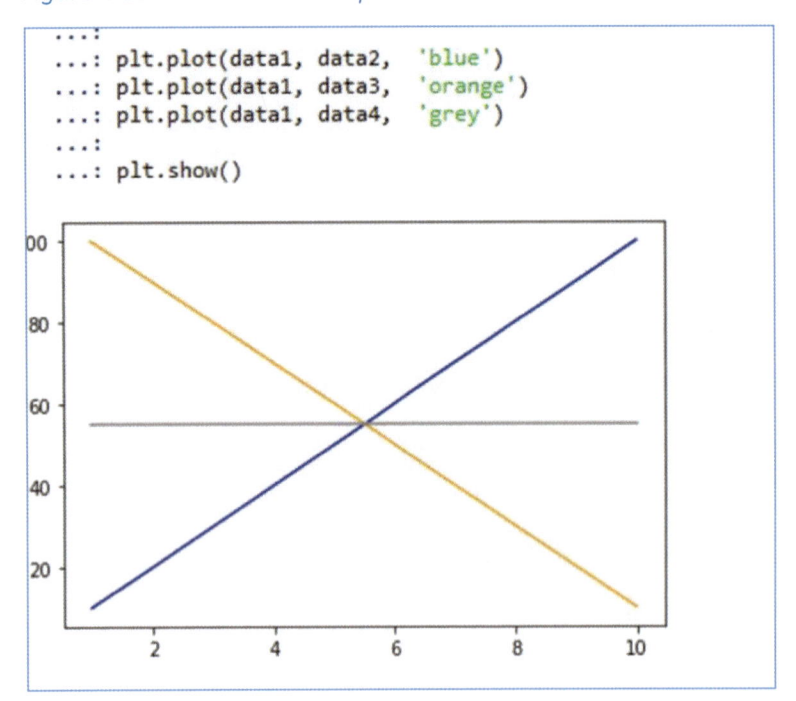

```
...: plt.plot(data1, data2, 'blue')
...: plt.plot(data1, data3, 'orange')
...: plt.plot(data1, data4, 'grey')
...:
...: plt.show()
```

The graph is similar to the one completed in Excel (without titles).

Python is capable of creating numerous and fantastic types of graphs. This book does not delve too much into the graph world, so please do not expect fantastic graphs using Python within this book (as Excel can produce insightful graphs with relative ease).

4.4 Simple linear regression

Example 1.5.1 introduced the simple linear regression, this will be recreated using Python.

4.4.1 Example of simple linear regression

We want to test to see if there is a relationship between sponge thickness and its liquid absorbency. We have designed an experiment with different levels of sponge thickness, with the amount of liquid is absorbed. The results were recorded in table 4.3.

Table 4.3: Simple linear regression data

Sponge thickness (mm)	Absorbance (ml)
0.3	0.13
0.6	0.09
1.9	0.33
2.1	0.23
2.4	0.41
3.2	0.68
5.2	0.86
5.3	0.92
6	0.95
6.2	0.71
7.7	1.12

Within Python, the following steps will be conducted:
- Create arrays
    - In this book we will define an array as a variable that can store a list of values.
- Create the simple linear regression
- Create a graph with a labelled axis and title

Program 4-12: Create our arrays

```
x = np.array([0.3, 0.6, 1.9, 2.1, 2.4, 3.2, 5.2, 5.3, 6, 6.2, 7.7]).reshape((-1, 1))
y = np.array([0.13, 0.09, 0.33, 0.23, 0.41, 0.68, 0.86, 0.92, 0.95, 0.71, 1.12])
```

np.array, tells Python that we want to create arrays using the figures within ([…])

Now, we have two arrays: the input x and output y. For regression to work within Python we need to amend x to be two-dimensional, one columns, but many rows. That's why we needed the command **reshape((-1,1))**.

Arrays allow us to manipulate data easier.

Program 4-13: Our simple linear regression code

```
from sklearn.linear_model import LinearRegression
# regresion code
model = LinearRegression()
model.fit(x, y)


#run code to get key statistics
intercept=model.intercept_
coef = model.coef_
r_sq = model.score(x, y)
```

1) Import a new library
2) Our regression code
3) Produces our output for the model –see figure 4.16

Figure 4.16: Our model

```
...: model = LinearRegression()
...: model.fit(x, y)
...:
...: intercept=model.intercept_
...: coef =  model.coef_
...: r_sq = model.score(x, y)
...:
...: print(intercept)
...: print(coef)
...: print(r_sq)
0.06684069929654801
[0.139236]
0.9095361017908764
```

Further information regarding simple linear regression will be explored later in the book (Chapter 8).

The next stage requires us to create the plot.

Program 4-14: Plotting simple linear regression model code

```
# create our predicted results -1
pred_y = (x * 0.13923 ) +0.066840


#create our plot -2
#create our plot
plt.plot(x, y,  'orange')
plt.plot(x, pred_y,  'blue')


# Add title and axis names
plt.title('Simple linear Regression')
plt.xlabel('Sponge (mm)')
plt.ylabel('absorbance (ml)')


plt.show()
```

1) We have created a new data array based on the model coefficients. This was done so we can plot our predicted value against our actual vales (trendline)
2) Our plotting code. More code has been added from previous examples
    a. plt.title('...') – puts the chart title
    b. plt.xlabel('...') –labels the x-axis
    c. plt.ylable('...') – labels the y-axis

Figure 4.17: Chart of simple linear regression with trendline

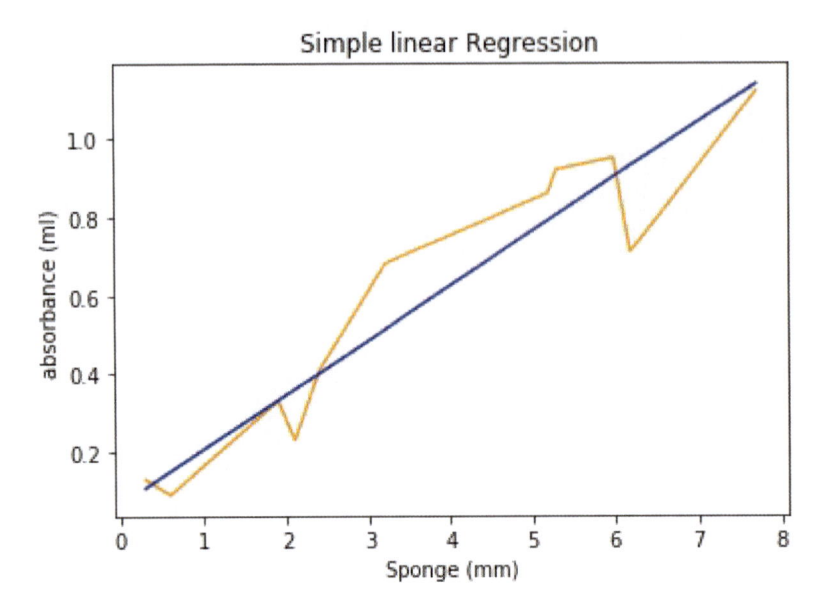

4.5 T-tests

The next section of our very quick introduction to Python involves solving the t-test exercise from example 2.1.

In this example, we want to test the effectiveness of a new drug. You ask some students their well-being (score 0 to 20), then without telling them, you start giving them this new drug. After a week you ask the same people their well-being. The results were recorded as shown in table 4.4.

Table 4.4: Example 2.1 data

Well-being pre-treatment	Well-being post-treatment
3	5
0	1
6	5
7	7
4	10
3	9
2	7
1	11
4	8

1. Calculate the mean & standard deviation
2. Are they correlated?
3. Calculate the t-test value to monitor if there has been a difference in the students' well-being.

Notes are very useful when coding:

- They provide you with a quick summary of what the code executes, without you needing to read through lines of code
- Allows your co-workers to understand your work.

Figure 4.40 displays the stages required for this exercise within R.

Figure 4.18: Creating arrays for t-test

```
83
84 # 1 create data arrays
85 # 2 calculate mean and standard deviation
86 # 3 Arre they correlated
87 # 4 Calculate the t-test
88
89 pre = np.array([3, 0, 6, 7, 4, 3, 2, 1, 4])
90 post = np.array([5, 1, 5, 7, 10, 9, 7, 11, 8])
91
```

To conduct the t-tests, the following steps will be required:
- Create the arrays with the values
    - pre
    - post
- Calculate the mean and standard deviation
- Calculate the correlation statistic
- Calculate the t-test statistic with a new command.

Hopefully, you will have found a pattern emerging with this very hands-on introduction to Python.
- Create the data
- Conduct the required statistics

Program 4-15: Initial statistical analysis

```
#1 our data arrays
pre = np.array([3,0,6,7,4,3,2,1,4])
post = np.array([5,1,5,7,10,9,7,11,8])

#2 our statistics
np.mean(pre)
np.mean(post)
```

Table 4.5: Initial results

	Well-being pre-treatment	Well-being post-treatment
Average	3.3333	7.0000
Standard deviation	2.2361	3.0414
Correlation	0.1470	

Program 4-16: T-test statistic

```
#import library
from scipy import stats

#t-test code
```

- **stats.ttest_ind(** - our command for Python to conduct t-test
- **pre, post,** - the data
- **equal_var = False)** – set to false, which does not assume equal population variance

Ttest_indResult(statistic=-2.9139711855430965, pvalue=0.010872301185460153)

The t-tests compare the two means and inform you if they are different from each other. They also tell you how significant they are or, in other words, whether it happened by chance.

- T = -2.91397
    - This is the t-score and is the ratio between the difference of the two groups and the difference between these groups.
- P-value (this is the value calculated in Excel)
    - Informs you of the probability whether the results from the sample occurred by chance or not. A P-value of 0.05 tells you that there is a 5% chance that the results occurred by chance. The lower the p-value, better the result. In this case, 0.108 signifies that the results have a 1.08% chance of occurring by chance.

Python uses a different t-test scenario than Excel, thus this difference in figures, but the results are similar.

4.6 Chi-square

The next exercise builds on the previous examples, as well as introducing new commands and a new data structure (program 5 chi-square). The following solves example 2.4.1.

2.4.1 Example of chi-square

We go for a walk in a lovely forest and comment on the colour of the apples. We expect to see ¾ red apples and ¼ green apples. After counting the apples in the forest, the results were recorded.

Table 4.6: Data for chi-square analysis

Apple Colour	observed	Expected
Red	545	547.5
Green	185	182.5
total	730	730

Excel formula:

=CHITEST (observed range, expected range)

As before, our first step is to create our arrays

Program 4-17: Chi-square, part 1 create our arrays

```
observed = np.array([545, 185])
expected = np.array([547.5, 182.5])
```

The next stage is to convert our arrays into a data frame. A data frame allows you to store data in a 2 dimensional way, rows and columns. Previously, our lists and arrays stored one column of data with numerous rows, using a data frame allows us to expand our data knowledge so that it includes numerous columns.

Program 4-18: Chi-square, part 2 convert arrays to data frame

```
chi_data = pd.DataFrame({'observed': observed, 'expected': expected})
```

Program 4-18 creates a data frame containing two columns and two rows:
- **Chi_data** - name of our data frame
- **pd.Dataframe** – command to create our data frame
- **'observed'** – create a column called observed
    - **:observed** – containing the data in the array observed
- **'expected'** – create a column called expected
    - **:expected** – containing the data in the array expected

Figure 4.19: Data frame chi_data

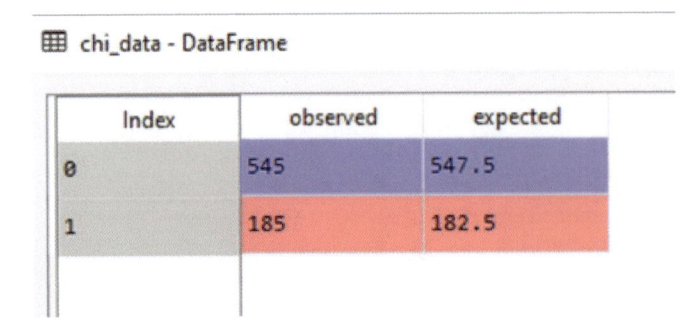

Index	observed	expected
0	545	547.5
1	185	182.5

Our last stage involves the following steps:
- Enabling the library
- Conducting the chi-square test

Program 4-19: Chi-square, part 3 chi-square test

```
from scipy.stats import chi2_contingency
stats.chi2_contingency(chi_data)
```

- **stats.chi2_contingency** - the command used
- **(chi_data)** – our data frame

Figure 4.20: initial results

```
(0.008181945547097558, 0.9279263613756847, 1, array([[546.25, 546.25],
       [183.75, 183.75]]))
```

From the initial results, the results can be quite confusing:

- **0.00818** – this is our chi-square value
- **0.9279** – this is our p-value
- **1** - this is our degrees of freedom.
    - Degrees of freedom is calculated by using the **number of columns – 1 *(2-1)***.
- Last part is the expected results

Luckily, Python has an easier way to present the results

Program 4-20: Chi-square, part 4 chi-square test

```
chi2_stat, p_val, dof, ex = stats.chi2_contingency(chi_data)
```

Our first part of the code **chi2_stat, p_val, dof, ex**, tells Python to create 4 different objects, each containing the values. Therefore, to get our chi-square statistic, we do the following

Program 4-21: Chi-square, part 5 chi-square p-value

```
p_val
```

This produces our p_value of 0.9279, which is the same as Excel result.

As you start programming in Python, you will inevitably find more than one way to do any task. The choice should be yours, as long as the results produced are correct.

4.7 Summary

The main aim of this chapter was to get started in Python, without much theory. It demonstrates that to use Python intelligently, we have to install packages and libraries. Python is a programming language, which is why we used Excel to introduce some basic coding using commands and 'if' statements, so the leap into Python would not be so huge. No one becomes a master of a programming language overnight, it can take months/years and as usual patience and application are key. This does not mean that we should not use Python, just be patient as you learn.

5 Data for Python and data manipulation

No matter which analytical language you use, data is the most important aspect of any analysis. If your data was rubbish, then any analysis produced would be rubbish. One of the most common sayings in the analytical world is

> RUBBISH IN = RUBBISH OUT

When people focus on techniques rather than data, they will produce unrealistic results with confusing conclusions. Understanding your data and how it should behave is key in analytics. This will become more apparent when we start manipulating data.

This chapter delves further into data and data structure.

5.1 Basic data types in Python

Python basic formats:

- Boolean
    - True, False
- Numeric
    - Integer e.g. 1, 2
    - Float e.g. 5.6
    - complex 6 - 2i)
- String
    - E.g., "BOB", "fun"
- Binary
    - 0, 1

In this book, we will mainly focus on integer, numeric and string (character) data types.

Python also has many data structures, but this book will focus on these three:

- list
- array
- data frame

We have used these different data structures in chapter 4.

5.1 The Data for chapter 5

Being able to clean and amend data is key to becoming a strong analyst. As you might have discovered with this book, a more hands-on approach than theory is used.

For this chapter, a CSV file called 'sample' is required. This file details the likelihood of a customer defaulting on a financial product.

Please import it, either through the Python importing data or writing the script yourself, for us to 'clean'.

Program 5-1: Importing CSV file

```
sample = pd.read_csv("C:/temp/sample.csv")
```

When we import this CSV file, it creates a data frame, called sample.
- **sample=**, the data frame we are creating
- **pd.read_csv(** - the command to read the CSV file
- **"C:/temp/sample.csv"** – where the file is stored, to be imported into Python

All of our work in this chapter will use this data frame.

This data frame has 13508 rows and 16 columns. The columns are described in table 5.1.

Table 5.1: Dataset description

Column number	Column Name	Column description
1	ID	Customer ID
2	Target	Whether the customer has become bankrupt
3	CCJ_government	Number of debts from the government (last 6 months)
4	CCJ_private	Number of debts from a private company (last 6 months)
5	bank_bal2	Second bank account balance
6	land_worth	Equity of land for sale
7	bank_balance	Main bank balance
8	Wages	Customer wages
9	house_value	Value of house difference from last year
10	Savings	Savings
11	amount_owed	Loans owed
12	wages_debt_percent	Total wages by total debt percentage
13	stocks_profile	Any stocks held
14	difference_wages_last_year	Percentage increase or decrease in wages last year
15	Properties	Properties owned
16	Mortgage	Number of properties with a mortgage

Our first task would have a look at the top 20 rows. To do this, we will create a new data frame called top20, containing the first 20 rows of the data frame, sample.

Program 5-2: viewing top 20 rows of sample

```
top20 = sample.head(20)
```

- **top20-** name of the new data frame
- **sample** – name of our data frame
- **head(20)** – head is the command telling Python that we want to view the top number of rows. The number 20, tells Python that we want the top 20 rows.

Then just double click on this new data frame (in variable explorer pane). If using Jupyter, then we can just write **top20.**

Figure 5.1: Variable Explorer pane

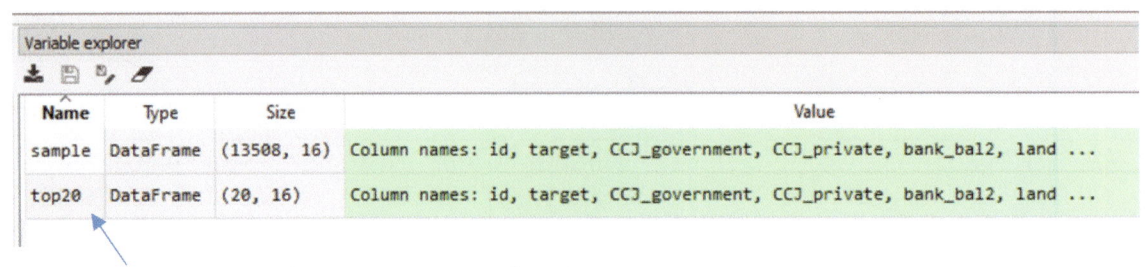

Name	Type	Size	Value
sample	DataFrame	(13508, 16)	Column names: id, target, CCJ_government, CCJ_private, bank_bal2, land ...
top20	DataFrame	(20, 16)	Column names: id, target, CCJ_government, CCJ_private, bank_bal2, land ...

Double clicking here will open up our new data frame.

Figure 5.2: Data frame top 20

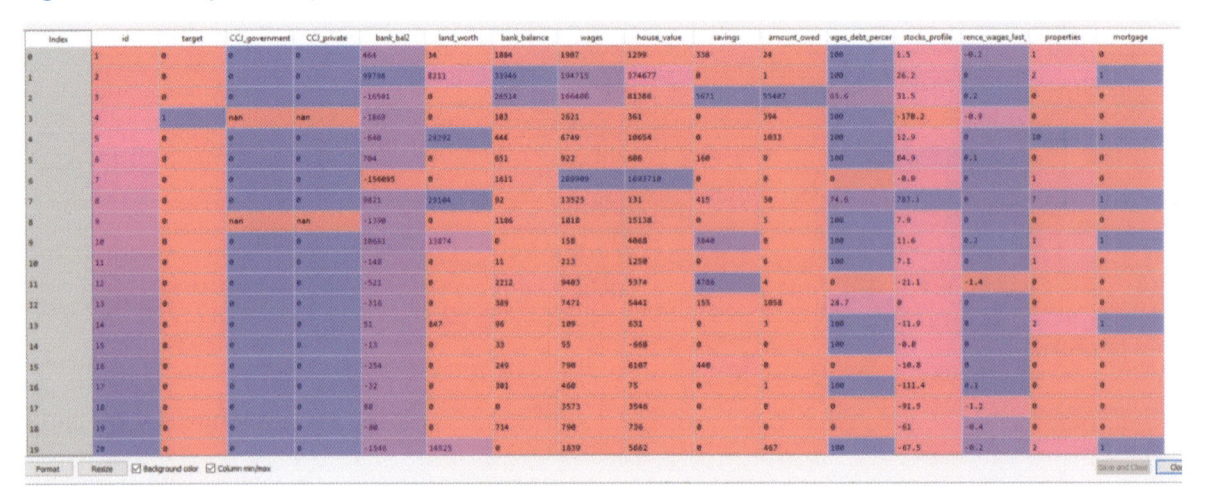

- The first thing to notice is that the index column starts on number 0.
- Secondly, 2 columns have had their missing value changed from blank (missing) to **nan** (CCJ_governmet and CCJ_private)

Python overwrites missing values with *nan*. Treating missing values is covered in the next section.

To close this window, we just click the 'x' in the right hand corner of the data frame.

The next stage involves obtaining the data about the data (metadata). To get this information we use:

Program 5-3: Sample metadata

```
sample.info()
```

Metadata involves the data about the data, in Python we use **.info()**, where the data frame name precedes this.

Figure 5.3: info()

```
In [32]: sample.info()
<class 'pandas.core.frame.DataFrame'>
RangeIndex: 13508 entries, 0 to 13507
Data columns (total 16 columns):
id                           13508 non-null int64
target                       13508 non-null int64
CCJ_government               12416 non-null float64
CCJ_private                  12416 non-null float64
bank_bal2                    13508 non-null int64
land_worth                   13508 non-null int64
bank_balance                 13508 non-null int64
wages                        13508 non-null int64
house_value                  13508 non-null int64
savings                      13508 non-null int64
amount_owed                  13508 non-null int64
wages_debt_percent           13508 non-null float64
stocks_profile               13402 non-null float64
difference_wages_last_year   13402 non-null float64
properties                   13508 non-null int64
mortgage                     13508 non-null int64
dtypes: float64(5), int64(11)
```

From the info() command, we can see that the data frame sample has:

- 13508 obs (rows)
- 16 variables (columns)
- The names of all of the variables (these are case-sensitive)
- The variables are either integers(int64) or numbers (float64)

This has given us further insight into the data that the **head()** command is not able to convey.

5.3 Data manipulation

Being able to amend data and only choosing specific values form a column is a key skill for any analyst/decision scientist.

5.3.1 Equal to

If we wanted to create a new data frame that contained only those customers that had become bankrupt (target=1), then we would write a little program. In Python, if we want a variable to equal a value, then we would use two equal signs '=='.

Program 5-4: Equal to

```
targ1 = sample[sample.target==1]
targ1.info()
```

The code has been broken down as follows:
- targ1 - the name of the new data frame created
- sample - the name of the data frame that we are going to interrogate
- [sample$target - informs Python the data frame and the variable we want to use
- == 1 – as mentioned previously, in Python we would use '==' to mean equal to
-] - specifies the end of the command

In Python column names and data frames are case sensitive, therefore 'Target' would not work, whereas 'target' does.

The info() command has been included for completeness, but we do not have to run it.

If we look at the top right-hand window, we will see that targ1 data frame has 1121 observations (figure 5.5).

Figure 5.4: Using the environment pane

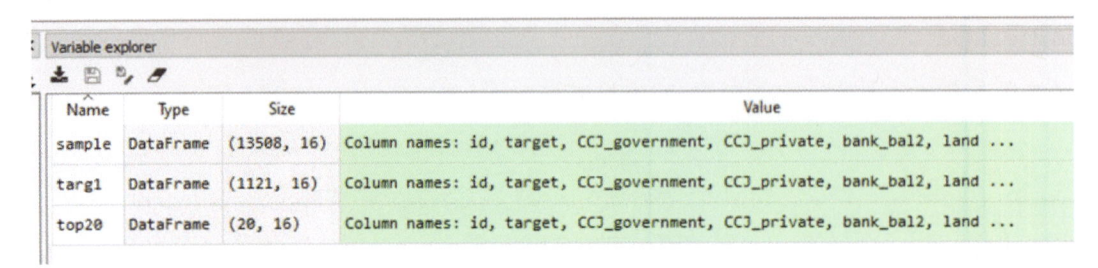

Name	Type	Size	Value
sample	DataFrame	(13508, 16)	Column names: id, target, CCJ_government, CCJ_private, bank_bal2, land ...
targ1	DataFrame	(1121, 16)	Column names: id, target, CCJ_government, CCJ_private, bank_bal2, land ...
top20	DataFrame	(20, 16)	Column names: id, target, CCJ_government, CCJ_private, bank_bal2, land ...

If you click on the word 'targ1', then, in Python this will display the data frame (figure 5.5)

Figure 5.5: Using the variable explorer pane

targ1 - DataFrame

Index	id	target	CCJ_government	CCJ_private	bank_
3	4	1	nan	nan	-1869
33	34	1	0	0	779
78	79	1	nan	nan	-2606
79	80	1	nan	nan	-327
82	83	1	nan	nan	-6032
84	85	1	0	0	6
104	105	1	2	0	-45
111	112	1	10	4	-96
145	146	1	nan	nan	-151
155	156	1	nan	nan	0
161	162	1	1	0	-72

5.3.2 Further expressions

So far we have seen the '==' command, but there are other commands:

Table 5.2: Further expressions

Symbol	Meaning	Example
==	Equal to	targ1 = sample[sample.target==1]
!=	Not equal to	targn1 = sample[sample.target != 1]
>	Greater than	wages1k = sample[sample.wages>1000]
<	Less than	save100 = sample[sample.savings <100]
>=	Greater than or equal to	Wages2k = sample[sample.wages>=2000]
<=	less than or equal to	Save500 = sample[sample.savings <=500]

Program 5-5: Other expressions

```
# where target =1
targ1 = sample[sample.target==1]


# where target not equal 1
targn1 = sample[sample.target != 1 ]


#where wages are greater than 1000
wages1k = sample[sample.wages>1000]


# where savings are less than 100
save100 = sample[sample.savings <100 ]
```

Figure 5.6: Basic expressions results

Name	Type	Size	Value
Save500	DataFrame	(11947, 16)	Column names: id, target, CCJ_government, CCJ_private, bank_bal2, land ...
Wages2k	DataFrame	(2801, 16)	Column names: id, target, CCJ_government, CCJ_private, bank_bal2, land ...
sample	DataFrame	(13508, 16)	Column names: id, target, CCJ_government, CCJ_private, bank_bal2, land ...
save100	DataFrame	(9463, 16)	Column names: id, target, CCJ_government, CCJ_private, bank_bal2, land ...
targ1	DataFrame	(12387, 16)	Column names: id, target, CCJ_government, CCJ_private, bank_bal2, land ...
targn1	DataFrame	(12387, 16)	Column names: id, target, CCJ_government, CCJ_private, bank_bal2, land ...
top20	DataFrame	(20, 16)	Column names: id, target, CCJ_government, CCJ_private, bank_bal2, land ...
wages1k	DataFrame	(5183, 16)	Column names: id, target, CCJ_government, CCJ_private, bank_bal2, land ...

Please note that the results are not in created order but in alphabetical order, where capital characters come before lower case ones.

It is common to manipulate data using two or more variables, which leads us to the 'and' and 'or' commands.

Using our data frame 'sample', we are going to create a new data frame that contains only those customers whose wages are over 2000 **and** have savings less than 100. In this scenario, we would use '&' and use each command with brackets, as shown below.

Program 5-6: AND command

```
wagesandsave = sample[(sample.wages >2000) & (sample.savings <100) ]
```

If we were to consider wages>3000 **or** savings>500 then we would use '|'.

Program 5-7: OR command

```
wagesorsave = sample[(sample.wages>3000 ) | (sample.savings> 500)]
```

Figure 5.7: Results from 'and' and 'or'

targ1	DataFrame	(12387, 16)	Column names: id, target, CCJ_government, CCJ_private, bank_bal2, land ...
targn1	DataFrame	(12387, 16)	Column names: id, target, CCJ_government, CCJ_private, bank_bal2, land ...
top20	DataFrame	(20, 16)	Column names: id, target, CCJ_government, CCJ_private, bank_bal2, land ...
wages1k	DataFrame	(5183, 16)	Column names: id, target, CCJ_government, CCJ_private, bank_bal2, land ...
wagesandsave	DataFrame	(1190, 16)	Column names: id, target, CCJ_government, CCJ_private, bank_bal2, land ...
wagesorsave	DataFrame	(2621, 16)	Column names: id, target, CCJ_government, CCJ_private, bank_bal2, land ...

As we can see from figure 5.10 the data frames have been created, but how can we check if they are correct? We can either do a quick 'eyeball' check by using head() or conduct some simple statistics as shown in table 5.3.

Table 5.3: Simple statistics code

Code	Result
np.min(wages1k.wages)	1001
np.max(save100.savings)	99
np.min(Wages2k.wages)	2000
np.max(Save500.savings)	500
np.min(wagesandsave.wages)	2003
np.max(wagesandsave.savings)	99

Note that data frames and column names are case sensitive, so if you have used capital letters in your coding (e.g. Save500), remember to continually use them.

We have extended our work from chapter 4 to calculating simple statistics using data frames. As long as the data frame and the variable (separated by '.') are written correctly, it is straightforward.

5.3.3 Exercise 5.1: basic commands

Using the data frame 'sample' complete the following activities:

1) Create a new data frame called activ1, using the data from sample where the target variable is equal to 0

2) Create a new data frame called activ2, using the data from sample where wages are greater than 5000

3) Create a new data frame called activ3 using the data from sample where wages are greater than or equal to 10000

4) Create a new data frame called activ4, using the data from sample where wages are less than or equal to 10000 and the target is not equal 0

5.3.4 Solution to exercise 5.1

Program 5-8: Solution to exercise 5.1

```
activ1 = sample[sample.target==0]
activ2 = sample[sample.wages>5000]
activ3 = sample[sample.wages>=10000]
activ4 = sample[(sample.wages <10000) & (sample.target != 0) ]
```

5.3.5 Characteristic variables

So far we have only considered numerical values, but data usually arrives in a mixture of characteristic and numerical values.

The first stage is to create a data frame with characteristic values:

Program 5-9: Character data frame

```
boom = np.array(["THIS", "IS", "AN", "EXAMPLE", "OF", "A", "CHARACTER", "DATA", "FRAME"])
bosh = pd.DataFrame({'boom': boom})
```

The above creates an array called 'boom', which is then converted into a data frame called 'bosh' using the command 'pd.DataFrame'.

To filter data by a characteristic variable is very similar to the numerical version as shown in in the following program

Program 5-10: Character variable data manipulation

```
#1 EQUALS TO
char1 = bosh[bosh.boom == "EXAMPLE"]


#2 NOT EQUALS TO
char2 = bosh[bosh.boom != "EXAMPLE"]


#3 or
char3 = bosh[(bosh.boom=="THIS" ) | (bosh.boom=="OF")]


# 4 multiple or
```

1) char1 = bosh[bosh.boom == "EXAMPLE"]
    a. We can use single or double quotes, but you must remember to <u>use</u> them and do not mix them e.g. "EXAMPLE' would not work
2) Same as number 1, but using non-equals
3) Again, as shown previously with the numerical version, but the words are surrounded by quotes.
4) Multiple or statements
    a. This demonstrates that we can use multiple **'or'** statements
5) This uses a short-cut from writing out the same variable numerous times. In this case, we can use the **'isin'** command, which provides us with the same result as in 5.

Figure 5.8: Results using characteristic variables

```
In [40]: char1
Out[40]:
       boom
3   EXAMPLE

In [41]: char2
Out[41]:
         boom
0        THIS
1          IS
2          AN
4          OF
5           A
6   CHARACTER
7        DATA
8       FRAME

In [42]: char3
Out[42]:
    boom
0   THIS
4     OF

In [43]: char4
Out[43]:
    boom
0   THIS
4     OF
7   DATA

In [44]: char5
Out[44]:
    boom
0   THIS
4     OF
7   DATA

IPython console    History log
```

The **isin** statement can be used for numerical as well as characteristic values. When dealing with characteristic variables you must remember that it is case sensitive e.g. from the previous example, char1 = bosh[bosh.boom == "EXAMpLE"] would not work.

5.4 Data frame manipulation in Python

5.4.1 Updating null values

When working with data, it rarely arrives ready to use (clean). In this scenario, you will be cleaning data to make it usable. From figure 5.2, it was observed that there are some missing values for CCJ_government and CCJ_private. (NA). Three common causes of missing values are:

- Unknown
- Data file imported incorrectly
- Unsuccessful match rates

The variables CCJ_government and CCJ_private contains missing values as they have never had any CCJ's. For these columns, we replace the missing values with 0.

The code below demonstrates how it was completed

Program 5-11: Updating null values

```
sample['CCJ_government'] = sample['CCJ_government'].fillna(0)

sample['CCJ_private'] = sample['CCJ_private'].fillna(0)
```

Segmenting the code:
- sample['CCJ_government'] =
    - specifies the data frame and the column we are amending/creating
- sample['CCJ_government'].
    - specifies the data frame and the column we are investigating
- fillna(0)
    - Change the NA to zero

This was then repeated for CCJ_private

Check the results with double clicking on sample

Figure 5.9: Pre-post results of amending null values

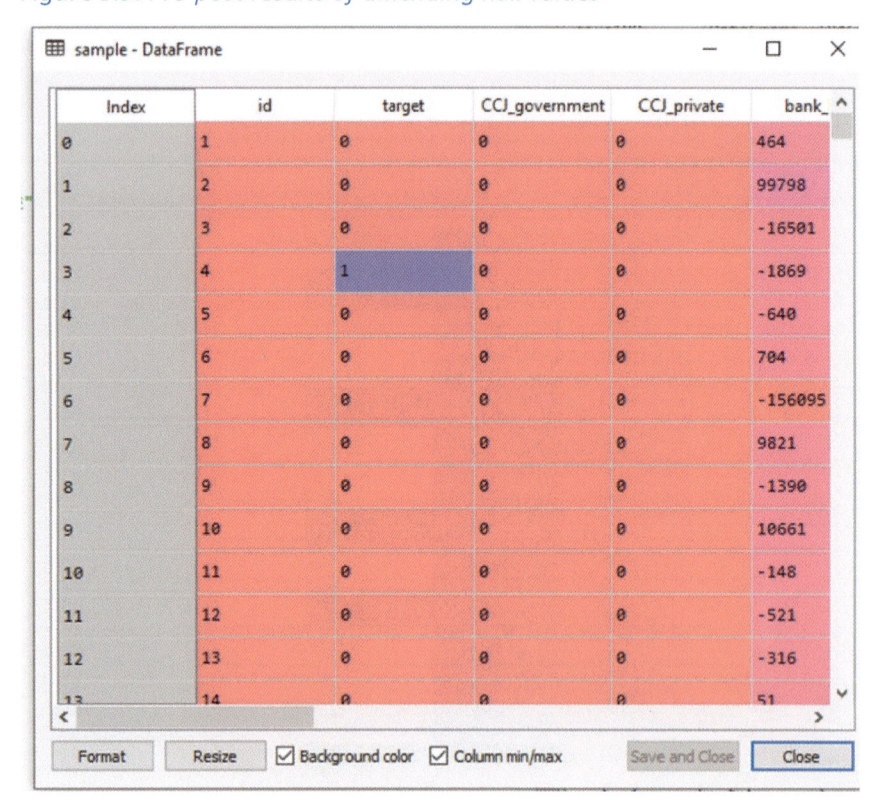

Index	id	target	CCJ_government	CCJ_private	bank_
0	1	0	0	0	464
1	2	0	0	0	99798
2	3	0	0	0	-16501
3	4	1	0	0	-1869
4	5	0	0	0	-640
5	6	0	0	0	704
6	7	0	0	0	-156095
7	8	0	0	0	9821
8	9	0	0	0	-1390
9	10	0	0	0	10661
10	11	0	0	0	-148
11	12	0	0	0	-521
12	13	0	0	0	-316
13	14	0	0	0	51

5.4.2 Creating new columns

The ability to create new columns is a key skill for an analyst. Sometimes, we may want to add a single value to the data frame or create a new column based on information already held in the data frame. The first example is to create a new column with the value 1 called count, within the data frame sample.

Program 5-12: Creating a new column

```
sample['count'] = 1
```

This is one of those scenarios where writing out what we are going to do is longer than the code itself. Just remember to write the data frame first, followed by the column name with ['..'] As usual, remember to run the code.

If we would like to add a date column to our data frame then we just use the pandas library and **to_datetime** command.

Program 5-13: Creating a date column

```
sample['date'] = pd.to_datetime('2020-02-02')
```

Next part involves creating a new variable (column) based on values from different variables in the data frame, sample. A new column called 'totalbank' will be created, which sums up the total bank balances in the data frame.

Program 5-14: Creating a new column based on other columns

```
sample['totalbank'] = (sample.bank_balance + sample.bank_bal2)
```

Hopefully, the code makes perfect sense to you, as all we are doing is creating a new column, which is based upon another column. Please note, that you have to specify the data frame for the new column and remember that it's case sensitive, but that should be the only difficulty. If you make a mistake, this is not an issue at this stage, as Python will just overwrite the column with the correct version when you re-run the correct version of the code.

5.4.3 Where

The 'where' command is very powerful, as it allows you to manipulate data effortlessly. This section will provide 2 examples of using the 'where' command to enable you to understand its flexibility. We have used the 'If' statement within Excel during 'section 3.2.2 if function', so you may find the logic familiar.

First of all, we are going to create a new variable (column) that contains the utilisation of debt(amount_owed) by savings. Usually, debt has a higher % rate than the savings rate.

As before we will create a new column.

Program 5-15: Creating a new column based on other columns-2

```
sample['amtowesav'] = (sample.amount_owed / sample.savings )
```

From the above example, we can see that we have created a new column called 'amtowesav', which is calculated by dividing amount_owed by savings.

If we were to look into this new variable we will notice the following.

Figure 5.10: Results of adding new columns to sample data frame

Index	properties	mortgage	count	date	totalbank	amtowesav
0	1	0	1	2020-02-02 00:00:00	2348	0.0710059
1	2	1	1	2020-02-02 00:00:00	133744	inf
2	0	0	1	2020-02-02 00:00:00	10013	9.77023
3	0	0	1	2020-02-02 00:00:00	-1686	inf
4	10	1	1	2020-02-02 00:00:00	-196	inf
5	0	0	1	2020-02-02 00:00:00	1355	0
6	1	0	1	2020-02-02 00:00:00	-154484	nan
7	7	1	1	2020-02-02 00:00:00	9913	0.0722892
8	0	0	1	2020-02-02 00:00:00	-204	inf
9	1	1	1	2020-02-02 00:00:00	10661	0
10	1	0	1	2020-02-02 00:00:00	-137	inf
11	0	0	1	2020-02-02 00:00:00	1691	0.000835771
12	0	0	1	2020-02-02 00:00:00	73	6.82581
13	2	1	1	2020-02-02	147	inf

Our new column has 'Inf' stored within it, as well as nan. This means infinity, as we have divided a number by zero. A simple way to solve this issue is to only calculate this ratio when the savings does not equal 0. This leads to using the **where** command.

Rather than giving the theory, this book will demonstrate how they are used with an example.

Program 5-16: Using np.where command

```
sample['amtowesav'] =np.where(sample.savings !=0, sample.amount_owed / sample.savings, 0)
```

- sample['amtowesav'] < -
    - This is the name of our new column within the data frame
- np.where(sample.savings !=0, sample.amount_owed / sample.savings, 0)
    - np.where – the new command, which works very similar to the Excel command 'IF'
    - savings != 0, - informs Python that whenever saving does not equal 0, then do the following
    - sample.amount_owed / sample.savings - the calculation we want completed
    - , 0)) – all those where savings does equal 0, put 0 in the column 'amtowesav'. This is then followed by the bracket.

Figure 5.11: Correcting infinity calculations

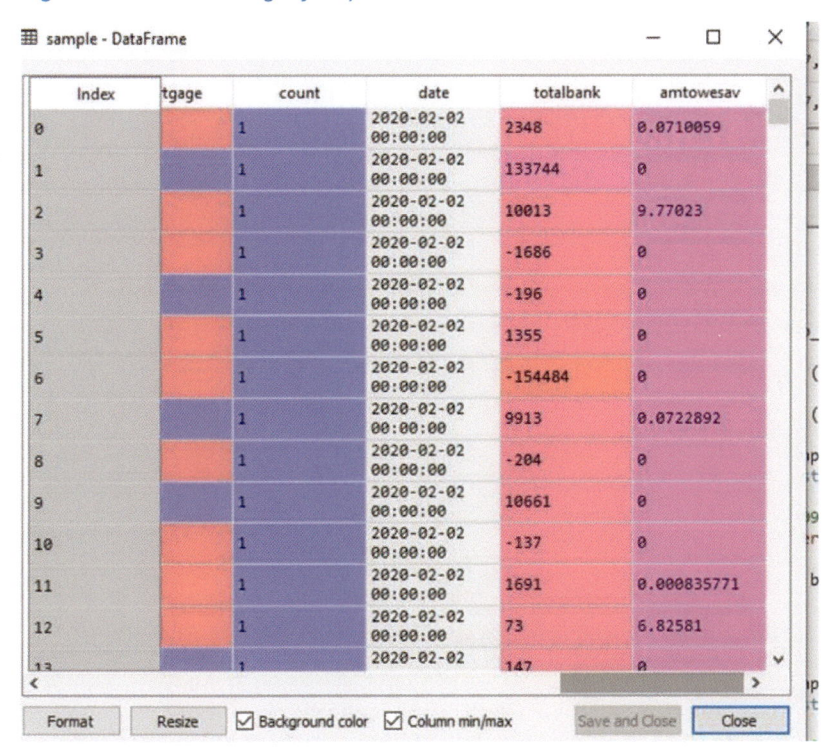

From the above, we can see that 'amtowesav' has a long string of decimals. Just for completeness, but which is not necessary, we can round this figure to one decimal place.

Program 5-17: Rounding numbers

```
sample['amtowesav'] = round(sample['amtowesav'], 1)
```

Figure 5.12: Rounding values in columns

If you would prefer 3 decimal places, then just replace the '1' with a '3'.

Just as a final note regarding the new variable.

The next part requires creating a new column called wageband, using the values within the column wages.

Program 5-18: Creating a categorical column based on another column

```
sample['wageband'] = np.where(sample.wages<100, 'low',
        np.where(sample.wages<1000, 'medium',
        np.where(sample.wages>=1000, 'high', 'err')))
```

- sample['wageband'] <-
    - Tells Python to create a new column called wageband in the data frame sample
- np.where(
    - The command to specify the criteria of the new column based on the available data
- sample.wages<100, 'low',
    - If wages are less than 100, then put 'low' in the new column 'wageband'. The inverted commas will not appear in the column.
- np.where(sample.wages<1000, 'medium',
    - If wages are less than 1000, then put 'medium'. Please note that it will not overwrite the first rule, (under 100) as it will process this command in order. Additionally, note that we have not used a closed bracket yet!
- np.where(sample.wages>=1000, 'high', 'err')))
    - the last part of the code informs us that any figures that are equal to or greater than 1000, put 'high' in the new column.
    - 'err' tells Python that for any scenarios, where the specifications are not matched, put 'err' in the column. This would help us locate any bugs in our coding.
    - Finally, we finalise the command with the brackets (all 3 of them)

Figure 5.13: Results of 'np.where' command

Index	unt	date	totalbank	amtowesav	wageband
0		2020-02-02 00:00:00	2348	0.1	high
1		2020-02-02 00:00:00	133744	0	high
2		2020-02-02 00:00:00	10013	9.8	high
3		2020-02-02 00:00:00	-1686	0	high
4		2020-02-02 00:00:00	-196	0	high
5		2020-02-02 00:00:00	1355	0	medium
6		2020-02-02 00:00:00	-154484	0	high
7		2020-02-02 00:00:00	9913	0.1	high
8		2020-02-02 00:00:00	-204	0	high
9		2020-02-02 00:00:00	10661	0	medium
10		2020-02-02 00:00:00	-137	0	medium

5.4.4 Exercise 5.2: creating a new column

This exercise involves manipulating the columns **land_worth.**

1) Create a new column based on **land_worth** called **landbands** using the following logic
    a. Where land_worth is zero and less
    b. Where land_worth is above zero and less than 100
    c. Where land_worth is equal to 100 or more and less than 1000
    d. Where land_worth is equal to 1000 or more
2) Create your own labelling for these bands

NOTE – keep an eye on the number of brackets used and do not forget the commas.

Program 5-19: Solution to exercise 5.2

```
# solution to exercise
sample['landbands'] = np.where(sample.land_worth <=0, "0 and under",
            np.where(sample.land_worth<100, ">0 to 100",
            np.where(sample.land_worth <1000, ">=100 to <1000",
            np.where(sample.land_worth >=1000, "1000 or more",  'err'   ))))
```

Figure 5.14: Solution to exercise 5.2

Index	ate	totalbank	amtowesav	wageband	landbands
0	2-02-00	2348	0.1	high	>0 to 100
1	2-02-00	133744	0	high	1000 or more
2	2-02-00	10013	9.8	high	0 and under
3	2-02-00	-1686	0	high	0 and under
4	2-02-00	-196	0	high	1000 or more
5	2-02-00	1355	0	medium	0 and under
6	2-02-00	-154484	0	high	0 and under
7	2-02-00	9913	0.1	high	1000 or more
8	2-02-00	-204	0	high	0 and under
9	2-02-00	10661	0	medium	1000 or more
10	2-02-00	-137	0	medium	0 and under
11	2-02-00	1691	0	high	0 and under

Summary sheet

Table 5.4: Key Python commands summarised

Symbol	Meaning	Example
==	Equal to	targ1 = sample[sample.target==1]
!=	Not equal to	targn1 = sample[sample.target != 1]
>	Greater than	wages1k = sample[sample.wages>1000]
<	Less than	save100 = sample[sample.savings <100]
>=	Greater than or equal to	Wages2k = sample[sample.wages>=2000]
<=	less than or equal to	Save500 = sample[sample.savings <=500]
&	and	Wagesandv=sample[(sample.wages <10000) & (sample.target != 0)]
|	Or	char3 = bosh[(bosh.boom=="THIS") | (bosh.boom=="OF")]
Isin	Equivalent of multiple 'Or'	char5 = bosh[bosh.boom.isin (["THIS", "OF", "DATA"])]

A quick note from the author. This book may seem quite intensive as an introductory course, but its key aim is to lay down the key foundations in an applied manner. There is only really one way to learn how to program and that is by doing it. I have discovered that the sooner people start using any programming language, the easier it becomes and also allows you to enhance your knowledge further.

6. Data merging

It is a rare occurrence when all of your data requirements are available in one data frame. In this chapter, we will be creating a mock data frame based on the CSV file sample, to enable us to merge data and to introduce more commands within R.

This chapter covers the topics:
- Sampling
- Keeping/dropping columns from data frames
- Sorting data
- Merging data frames
    - Full join
    - Exclusive join
    - Concatenating/Appending

As previously mentioned, the application is more beneficial than theory work, therefore we proceed straight into developing new data frames.

6.1 Creating the mock frame

Please import the CSV file sample into Python.

Program 6-1: Importing data

```
import numpy as np
import pandas as pd

#import data
sample = pd.read_csv("C:/temp/sample.csv")
```

The next stage involves creating a data frame called mockdata which contains:

1) Two new variables
    a. Mock_wages, this is wages multiplied by 100
    b. Mock_savings, this is savings multiplied by 100
2) Another variable using the **np.where** command called Land_group
    a. Where land_worth is zero and less
    b. Where land_worth is above zero and less than 100
    c. Where land_worth is equal to 100 or more and less than 1000
    d. Where land_worth is equal to 1000 or more
3) A date field called Mock_date – 2002-02-02
4) The following variables
    a. Id
    b. Mock_wages
    c. Mock_savings
    d. Land_group
    e. Mock_date

If you decided to skip chapters 4 and 5 and start at this chapter, then this list of requirements could look daunting. If you hadn't, then you would be aware that we using our knowledge from previous chapters.

Part 1 – creating two new variables

Program 6-2: Creating two new variables

```
sample['mock_wages'] = sample.wages * 100
sample['mock_savings'] = sample.savings * 100
```

Part 2 – creating a new variable with **where**

Program 6-3: Creating a new variable with where

```
sample['land_group'] = np.where(sample.land_worth <=0, "0 and under",
                np.where(sample.land_worth<100, ">0 to 100",
                np.where(sample.land_worth <1000, ">=100 to <1000",
                np.where(sample.land_worth >=1000, "1000 or more", 'err'
```

Part 3 – creating a dated column

Program 6-4: Creating the mock_date column

```
sample['mock_date'] = pd.to_datetime('2020-02-02')
```

The final part of this exercise requires the data frame to only contain the following:

    a. Id

    b. Mock_wages

    c. Mock_savings

    d. Land_group

    e. Mock_date

Part 4– creating a mock data frame

Program 6-5: Selecting the columns

```
mockdata= sample[['id', 'mock_wages', 'mock_savings', 'land_group', 'mock_date']]
```

From the code above, we have created a data frame called **mockdata**, using just the columns chosen (in inverted commas) within [[...]]

Figure 6.1: Data frame mockdata

Index	id	mock_wages	mock_savings	land_group	mock_date
0	1	190700	33800	>0 to 100	2020-02-02 00:00:00
1	2	19471500	0	1000 or more	2020-02-02 00:00:00
2	3	16640800	567100	0 and under	2020-02-02 00:00:00
3	4	262100	0	0 and under	2020-02-02 00:00:00
4	5	674900	0	1000 or more	2020-02-02 00:00:00
5	6	92200	16000	0 and under	2020-02-02 00:00:00
6	7	28990900	0	0 and under	2020-02-02 00:00:00
7	8	1352500	41500	1000 or more	2020-02-02 00:00:00
8	9	181800	0	0 and under	2020-02-02 00:00:00
9	10	15800	384000	1000 or more	2020-02-02 00:00:00
10	11	21300	0	0 and under	2020-02-02 00:00:00
11	12	940300	478600	0 and under	2020-02-02 00:00:00

If we were to view all of those tasks in one go, then it could have been daunting. Due to the ability to break down the tasks into manageable pieces, it was easier to produce our final data frame (mockdata).

The next step involves selecting a random sample from mockdata and call it mockdata1. The command is called **sample**.

Program 6-5: Random selection of rows

```
mockdata1 = mockdata.sample(n = 1000)
```

The number (1000) informs Python the total number of rows(observations) we require. In this case, we are telling Python to provide us with a random 1000 rows from the data frame mockdata.

The final data frame created will be called mocksamp. This will only contain 3 columns from the data frame **sample**:
- Id
- Wages
- Mortgage

Program 6-6: Creating mocksamp

```
mocksamp =sample[['id', 'wages', 'mortgage']]
```

As before, selecting columns from a data frame mainly involves putting the data frame name outside the [[..]] and within the brackets, list the columns you want in inverted commas separated by commas.

6.2 Merging datasets

This section will only consider joining two data frames and will focus on three different types of joins:
- Full/Outer
- Exclusive
- Appending/concatenating

6.2.1 Full/Outer join

A full join uses all of the data from both sets of data and when there is data in one part and not in the other, then it will populate these values as 'missing'.

When explaining joins, we tend to use circles.

Figure 6.2: Diagram of a full join

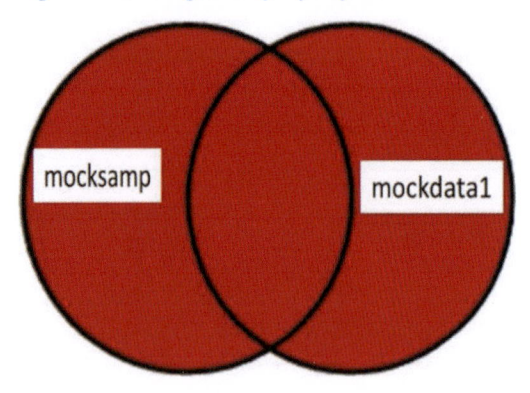

A full join means that we will use all of the data from mocksamp and mockdata1, even if there are observations in one dataset and none in the other.

Copy and run the code below

Program 6-7: Full/ Outer join

```
fulljoin = pd.merge(mocksamp, mockdata1, on='id', how='outer')
```

1) The command here is pd.merge
    a. This tells Python you want to merge data frames together
        i. mocksamp
            1. this gives the data frame an alias labelled 'x'.
        ii. mockdata1
            1. this gives the data frame an alias labelled 'y'.

2) on = "id"
    a. This tells Python the variable to merge the data with.

3) how='outer'
    a. This is a key command that tells Python the type of join you want to use. In this case, it is a full/outer join.

Figure 6.3: Full join result

Index	id	wages	mortgage	mock_wages	mock_savings	land_group	mock_date
0	1	1907	0	nan	nan	nan	NaT
1	2	194715	1	nan	nan	nan	NaT
2	3	166408	0	nan	nan	nan	NaT
3	4	2621	0	nan	nan	nan	NaT
4	5	6749	1	nan	nan	nan	NaT
5	6	922	0	nan	nan	nan	NaT
6	7	289909	0	nan	nan	nan	NaT
7	8	13525	1	nan	nan	nan	NaT
8	9	1818	0	nan	nan	nan	NaT
9	10	158	1	nan	nan	nan	NaT
10	11	213	0	nan	nan	nan	NaT
11	12	9403	0	nan	nan	nan	NaT
12	13	7471	0	747100	15500	0 and under	2020-02-02 00:00:00
13	14	109	1	nan	nan	nan	NaT
14	15	55	0	nan	nan	nan	NaT
15	16	790	0	nan	nan	nan	NaT

As we only took a random sample of 1000 rows from sample, we will end up with a lot of 'nan' (naT for date data) in the data frame, as shown in figure 6.5. There is a very good chance that your table will look different to figure 6.5, this is due to Python randomly selecting the 1000 rows. Do not worry about it, if there was an error, Python would tell you.

This is why it is called a **full join** as it contains **all** of the data. If there were rows in mockdata1 that was not in mocksamp, then we would see missing values (NA) for the variables from mocksamp.

6.2.2 Exclusive joins

Exclusive joins allow us to select data that was only relevant in one of the data frames, and where it matches in the other data frame. The following example will concentrate on the data frame mockdata1, and where there is a match on the dataset mocksamp, then it will use this data.

Figure 6.4: Diagram of an exclusive join

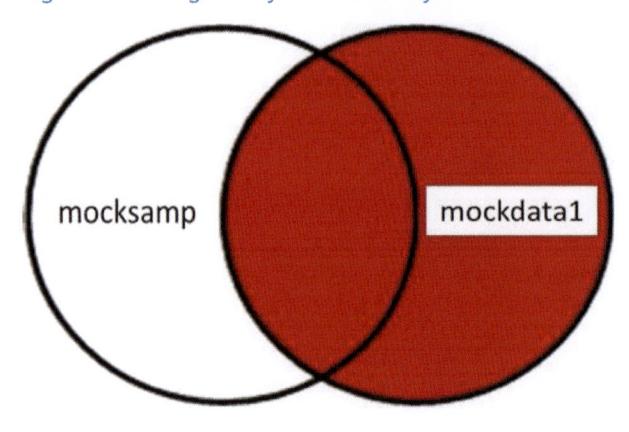

Program 6-8: Right join

```
rightjoin = pd.merge(mocksamp, mockdata1, on='id', how='right')
```

This code is very similar to program 6-7, with just the **how** statement being changed

Mocksamp contains 13508 rows, mockdata1 contains 1000 rows. As we only want values that are relevant in mockdata1, the code produces a data fame called 'rightjoin' with only 1000 rows (observations). For a left join, we would use **how='left'**

Another type of exclusive join is when you want to use data that appear in both datasets, in other words, where there are the same IDs in both tables. This is called an ***inner join.***

Figure 6.5: Diagram of exclusive join (2)

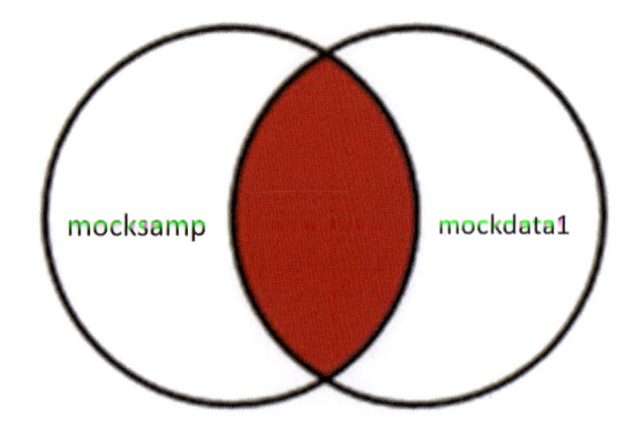

Program 6.9: Code for inner join

```
innerjoin = pd.merge(mockdata1, mocksamp, on='id', how='inner')
```

Once again, the code is very similar except for **how = 'inner'**. In this scenario, we would get 1000 rows (same as right join), this is because we have taken a random sample from mockdata to create mocksamp.

6.2.3 Concatenating/appending data

Sometimes we may have 2 datasets that we want to combine by stacking them one on top of the other, this is referred to either concatenating or appending.

Figure 6.6: Diagram of appending join

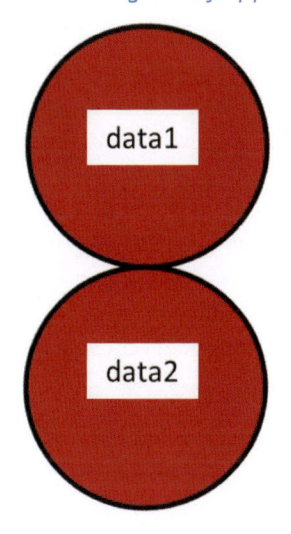

Program 6.10: Code for Concatenating join

```
conc = pd.concat([mocksamp, mockdata1])
```

The command to append the data is straightforward, **pd.concat.** This will produce a data frame called **conc** containing 14508 rows and 7 columns

Data preparation is very important when conducting the analysis. Chapter 5 provided the basic commands to clean data. Without simple data cleaning you may end up with wrong results and misleading figures being reported.

Additionally, rarely is the data you require stored in one place, thus the need to join tables, as described in chapter 6.

6.3 Summary

The table below contains the key pieces of code as shown in chapter 6.

Table 6.1: Chapter 6 sample code

Sample Code	Description
mocksamp =sample[['id', 'wages', 'mortgage']]	Selecting columns from a data frame
mockdata1 = mockdata.sample(n = 1000)	Taking a random sample of 1000 rows
fulljoin = pd.merge(mocksamp, mockdata1, on='id', how='outer')	Full join between 2 data frames
rightjoin = pd.merge(mocksamp, mockdata1, on='id', how='right')	Exclusive 'right join' code between two data frames
innerjoin = pd.merge(mockdata1, mocksamp, on='id', how='inner')	Exclusive 'inner join' code between two data frames
conc = pd.concat([mocksamp, mockdata1])	Appending/concatenating two data frames.

7 Analysis

This section provides the tools to start analysing data. As shown previously, data is rarely provided 'ready for use', so we have to know how to manipulate your data frames using specific commands.

Previously, we calculated simple statistics, now we will extend our knowledge into the analysis.

The following chapter demonstrates how we can use Python to conduct useful and insightful analysis and how we can use numerous tools to present the results.

Python has some powerful packages that allow us to carry out complex analysis, simplistically.

7.1 Introduction to analysing data

Previously, we used a pivot table to conduct analysis (section 3.3.1), this chapter will use Python. It is common to email reports with Excel attachments, but if we use raw instead of summarized data, we could be possibly sending out emails with 10s or 100s of megabytes in size. Python allows us to reduce the data size, to provide key information, which can then be used within Excel.

As previously, we will learn by application rather by theory.

7.1.1 Creating the dataset

The first stage involves using the data from sample.csv, with the following amendments:
- Overwrite the nan in CCJ_government to 0
- Overwrite the nan in CCJ_private to 0
- Create a column with the number 1

Program 7-1: Creating our data frame

```
import numpy as np
import pandas as pd
#import data
sample = pd.read_csv("C:/temp/sample.csv")
sample['count']=1
sample['CCJ_government'] = sample['CCJ_government'].fillna(0)
sample['CCJ_private'] = sample['CCJ_private'].fillna(0)
```

This code was copied and pasted from Chapter 5. A large amount of programming tends to involve copying, pasting and amending previous work. This is why it is good practice to leave insightful notes within your code. **REMEMBER TO RUN THIS CODE BEFORE PROCEEDING**

7.1.2 Basic analysis

Just as a recap, we will produce some simple statistics:
- Total number of customers with CCJ_private
- Average wages of the customers

Program 7-2: Simple statistics using a data frame

```
np.sum(sample.CCJ_private)
np.mean(sample.wages))
```

These commands are straightforward and produce the following results:
- Total CCJ_private =1237
- Average wages = 2269.99

7.2 Summarising data by groups

It is common to summarise data by grouping them by specific attributes to gather deeper insightful analysis e.g.
- The average age of males and females

7.2.1 Example of summarising data by groups

We want to analyse the total number of CCJs filed by the government, by those people who became bankrupt.

For this we will:

1. Create a new data frame called sum_exer
2. Use the target flag to create a new column called bankrupt
3. Summarise the data for our results

Steps 1 and 2 are straightforward and have been covered previously.

Program 7-3: Creating a new data frame and variable

```
sum_exe=sample
sum_exe['bankrupt'] = np.where(sum_exe.target==1, "YES", "NO")
```

The above tells Python that if target equals 1, then the column bankrupt equals "YES", else for all other rows, make bankrupt equal "NO".

For step 3, we will be summarizing by groups

Program 7-4: Creating a new data frame and variable

```
sum_exe.groupby(['bankrupt']).sum()[["count", "CCJ_government"]]
```

We have completed simple statistics before, program7-4 takes it to the next level
- sum_exe.groupby(['bankrupt']).
    - use the data frame **sum_exe**
    - **groupby(['bankrupt']).** – segment the following statistics by the variable bankrupt
- .sum()[["count", "CCJ_government"]]
    - **sum()** – add (sum) the following filed
    - **count** - adds up all the number 1
    - **CCJ-government** - adds all of the ccj_government figures

Figure 7.1: Results

```
        count  CCJ_government
bankrupt
NO      12387           518.0
YES      1121          2248.0
```

Tabulating the results for ease of reference produces:

Table 7.1: Table of Results

bankrupt	count	CCJ_government
NO	12387	518
YES	1121	2248

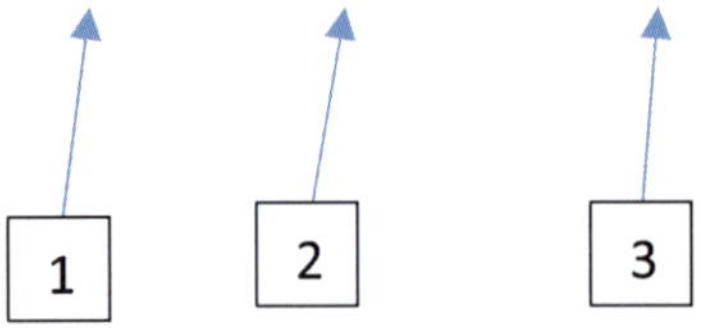

    1   2   3

1) bankrupt
    a. The variable that was segmented for the analysis
2) count
    a. This is the variable used as specified in the summarized statement and tells you the number of rows/observations were used from the data frame
        i. 12387 are not bankrupt
        ii. 1121 become bankrupt
3) CCJ_government
    a. This is the variable used as specified in the summarized statement
        i. 518 CCJ_government not bankrupt
        ii. 2248 CCJ_government bankrupt

From the results, we notice that CCJ_government is greater than the total of customers in that group. The following investigates this anomaly further.

7.3 Calculating percentages

7.3.1 Example of creating percentages

Building on what has been produced previously, we want to calculate the % of those with a CCJ go bankrupt. Additionally, the bankruptcy % figure for all the full population will also be calculated. Adhering to the methods so far in this book we will:

1. Create a data frame based on previous example (7.2.1)
2. Create new data frame based on the previous example without the 'group by'
    a. Create a new column called bankrupt, with the value "ALL"
3. Append both data frames to create a new data frame
4. Calculate the % on this new data frame

Amending the code used previously, we can quickly produce:

Program 7-5: solution to example 7.3.1

```
perc1 = sum_exe.groupby(['bankrupt']).sum()[["count", "CCJ_government"]]
perc1['all'] = 'all'


perc2 = perc1.groupby(['all']).sum()[["count", "CCJ_government"]]
perc2['bankrupt'] ='all'


perc3 = pd.concat([perc1, perc2])
perc3['percy'] = (perc3['CCJ_government'] / perc3['count'])
perc3
```

Note, to calculate the %, you can not use *perc3.CCJ_government/ perc3.count* as it will error!

Figure 7.2: Calculating percentages results

```
     CCJ_government  all  bankrupt  count      perc
NO            518.0  all       NaN  12387  0.041818
YES          2248.0  all       NaN   1121  2.005352
all          2766.0  NaN       all  13508  0.204768
```

The column perc has yet to have a % sign. This can be solved by:

- Multiplying by 100
- Converting the number into a **string**
- Adding a % sign at the end.

Additionally, to make the results more aesthetically pleasing, we will round the original calculation to 4 decimal places, which will give our % figures a 2 decimal point accuracy.

Program 7-6: Full solution to example 7.3.1

```
#step1 summarise data

perc1 = sum_exe.groupby(['bankrupt']).sum()[["count", "CCJ_government"]]

# step 2 add 'all' field
perc1['all'] = 'all'

#step 3 summarise by 'all'
perc2 = perc1.groupby(['all']).sum()[["count", "CCJ_government"]]
perc2['bankrupt'] ='all'

#step 4 concatenate
perc3 = pd.concat([perc1, perc2])
#step 5 calculate the %

perc3['perc'] = round(perc3['CCJ_government'] / perc3['count'],4)
 # step 6 presentation of percentage next
perc3.perc = (perc3.perc * 100).astype(str) + '%'


perc3
```

Figure 7.3: Full results to example 7.3.1

```
     CCJ_government  all bankrupt  count     perc
NO            518.0  all      NaN  12387    4.18%
YES          2248.0  all      NaN   1121  200.54%
all          2766.0  NaN      all  13508   20.48%
```

Results

Writing these results into a table produces

Table 7.2: Example 7.3 results

bankrupt	Count	CCJ_government	perc
NO	12387	518	4.18%
YES	1121	2248	200.54%
ALL	13508	2766	20.48%

　　1　　　　　2　　　　　3　　　　　4

1) Bankrupt
    a. The variable that was segmented for the analysis, the first column
2) Count
    a. This tells you the number of rows/observations were used from the dataset for the procedure.
3) CCJ_government
    a. This is the variable used as specified in the summarized statement
4) Perc
    a. The percentage calculation

As an analyst, you may have noticed that for bankrupt = 'YES', the percent is over 100%. A quick review of the data shows that some people have more than 1 CCJ, so these figures do not give a true figure of % of people with a government CCJ are bankrupt.

This is a valuable lesson, never make presumptions about the data

7.3.2 Exercise 7.1: summarising and percentages

Using the previous example create a new variable that has the following logic:
- if the total number of government CCJ is one or more, make it equal to 1, else make it equal 0.

This will require using the 'np.where' command.

Then, discover the true % of customers with a government CCJ that end up going bankrupt.

7.3.3 Solution to exercise 7.1

Program 7-7: Full solution to exercise 7-1

```
#exercise 7.1
#step 0 fix ccj_government
sum_exe7_1 = sample
sum_exe7_1['ccj_gov'] = np.where(sum_exe7_1.CCJ_government>=1, 1, 0)


#step1 summarise data
perc1 = sum_exe7_1.groupby(['bankrupt']).sum()[["count", "ccj_gov"]]


# step 2 add 'all' field
perc1['all'] = 'all'


#step 3 summarise by 'all'
perc2 = perc1.groupby(['all']).sum()[["count", "CCJ_government"]]
perc2['bankrupt'] ='all'


#step 4 concatenate
perc3 = pd.concat([perc1, perc2])
#step 5 calculate the %
```

Again tabulating the results for ease of reference...

Table 7.3: Exercise 7.1 results

bankrupt	count	ccjgov	perc
NO	12387	296	2.39%
YES	1121	591	52.72%
ALL	13508	887	6.57%

From table 7.3, over 52% of people who had a CCJ from the government became bankrupt.

You may have copied and pasted the code previously, with the new step added (program 7-7), or you could have coded everything from scratch. If you copied and pasted the code from previously, this is not cheating and rarely is there any extra credit from coding from scratch (except, possibly, at job interviews). It can be safe to presume, that sometimes 80% of a programmers' time is spent copying, pasting and amending the previous code. It is the knowledge of the function of the commands that make you a more rounded programmer.

7.4 Creating a simple management information (MI) report

Ultimately, managers need insightful figures that enable them to formulate intelligent decisions. This next session will expand our knowledge further to produce a simple and useful report. This will entail writing a significant amount of code and creating new data frames, using our previous experiences covered so far in this book.

7.4.1 Example of simple MI report

Create a report detailing, by bankruptcy and for all:
- Total number of people
- Average wages
- Number of private and government CCJs
- Average bank balance
- Average savings

Before providing a solution, please find enclosed a relevant piece of code. If we would like to summarise and calculate average in one line of code, then we can use the following

Program 7-8: Summarising and averaging

```
summar1 = sum_exe7_1.groupby(['bankrupt']).agg({'count':'sum', 'wages':'mean').reset_index()
```

- **summar1 = sum_exe7_1.groupby(['bankrupt']).**
    - This section should be familiar
- **agg({'count':'sum', 'wages':'mean').**
    - Previously we used **sum** outside the brackets, but by using **agg**, with the relevant commands, we can calculate the **sum** and **mean** in one
- **reset_index()**
    - in our previous examples, the column for bankrupt appeared in the index column, this difficult to define. By using this command, we will have a column called index

The report is to detail these figures only and clearly.

Solution on next page

Program 7-9: Exercise 7.4.1

```
#exercise 7.4.1
# a repeat of the above but with an extra column created
# step 1 create a new column called ccj_gov and ccj_priv in a data frame called sum_exer7_4
sum_exe7_4 = sample
sum_exe7_4['ccj_gov'] = np.where(sum_exe7_4.CCJ_government>=1, 1, 0)
sum_exe7_4['ccj_priv'] = np.where(sum_exe7_4.CCJ_private>=1, 1, 0)


#step2 summarise
#added on a new command mean!
summar1 = sum_exe7_4.groupby(['bankrupt']).agg({'count':'sum','ccj_gov':'sum','ccj_priv':'sum',
             'wages':'mean','bank_balance':'mean', 'savings':'mean' }).reset_index()
summar1['all'] = 'all'


#step 3 summarise by 'all'
summar2 = summar1.groupby(['all']).agg({'count':'sum','ccj_gov':'sum','ccj_priv':'sum',
             'wages':'mean','bank_balance':'mean', 'savings':'mean' }).reset_index()
summar2['bankrupt'] ='ALL'


#step 4 concatenate
summar3 = pd.concat([summar1, summar2])


#step 5 calculate the %
#package and library already stored, we can combine percent command into the calcuation
summar3['perc_govccj'] = round(summar3['ccj_gov'] / summar3['count']  ,4)
summar3['perc_privccj'] = round(summar3['ccj_priv'] / summar3['count']  ,4)
summar3['perc_govccj'] = (summar3['perc_govccj'] * 100).astype(str) + '%'
summar3['perc_privccj'] = (summar3['perc_privccj'] * 100).astype(str) + '%'
```

Figure 7.4: View of summar3

Index	all	bank_balance	bankrupt	ccj_gov	ccj_priv	count	savings	wages	perc_govccj	perc_privccj
0	all	700.135	NO	296	76	12387	292.609	2382.14	2.39%	0.61%
1	all	94.4032	YES	591	350	1121	31.3434	1030.71	52.72%	31.22%
0	all	397.269	ALL	887	426	13508	161.976	1706.43	6.5699999999...	3.15%

From figure 7.4:

- Customers who go bankrupt tend to
    - Have more government CCJs than average
    - Have more private CCJs than average
    - Have lower than average wages
    - Have lower than average bank balances
    - Have lower than average savings

As can be observed, the results are not really attention grabbing and managers tend to like simple figures with graphs.

Python is capable of creating some wonderful graphs, but many businesses are familiar with Excel graphs. Therefore, we will be using Excel to create our graphs.

Program 7-10: Exporting data to a csv file for Excel

```
#step 6 export to excel
summar3.to_csv("C:/temp/summar3.csv", index = False)
```

- **summar3** is our data frame
- **.to_csv** is the command
- **"C:/temp/summar3.csv",** the path (folder) where we want to save our CSV file
- **index = False,** tells Python that we do not want to export the index column

Figure 7.5: Exporting data into Excel

	A	B	C	D	E	F	G	H	I	J
1	all	bank_bala	bankrupt	ccj_gov	ccj_priv	count	savings	wages	perc_gov	perc_privccj
2	all	700.1351	NO	296	76	12387	292.6089	2382.143	2.39%	0.61%
3	all	94.40321	YES	591	350	1121	31.34344	1030.714	52.72%	31.22%
4	all	397.2692	ALL	887	426	13508	161.9762	1706.428	6.57%	3.15%

In Excel, you can easily change the column names and amend the way the data is presented to create a simple management information (MI) report e.g.

Figure 7.6: Simple MI report

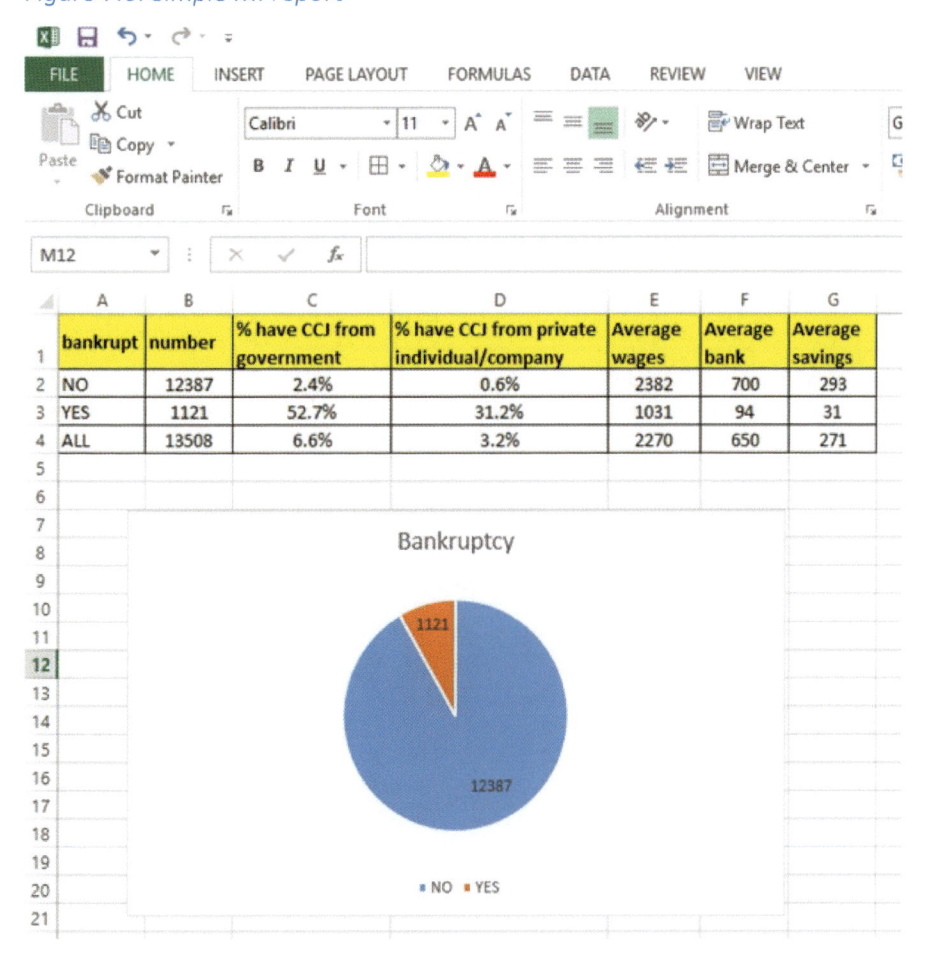

	A	B	C	D	E	F	G
1	bankrupt	number	% have CCJ from government	% have CCJ from private individual/company	Average wages	Average bank	Average savings
2	NO	12387	2.4%	0.6%	2382	700	293
3	YES	1121	52.7%	31.2%	1031	94	31
4	ALL	13508	6.6%	3.2%	2270	650	271

Bankruptcy pie chart: NO = 12387, YES = 1121

1) For the table, the following was conducted
    a. Renamed the columns
    b. Coloured the boxes
2) The pie chart was created using the same methodology as scatter chart as detailed in chapter 2

It took several minutes to create the report, without any further coding. There is no written rule that you have to use one programming language/software to achieve the final result.

Some people prefer to create the main data file with all of the summed figures, then use Excel to create averages, percentages etc…. This has been mentioned as Python is a great analytical tool that can handle huge datasets, but people may prefer to work out averages etc…after the dataset has been summarized.

Another reason why people prefer graphs in Excel is that they are easily manipulated and their appearance change requires little effort.

I have experienced many managers each wanting graphs created a specific way, from titles being written to a certain manner as well as the legend being from the side to the bottom, bar charts instead of lines… the list is quite exhaustive. In Excel, these graphs can be changed to the managers' requirements as they sit next to you, which makes the process smoother.

7.5 Exercise 7.2 creating a simple MI report using Python and Excel

The following exercise uses certain aspects from chapters 5 to 7. Please note that you can use old code to copy/paste and amend, it is only during interviews this is frowned upon.

7.5.1 Exercise 7.2: simple MI report

Create an MI report using the data from sample.csv by conducting the following:
- Import this data (if you have not already).
- Using this data frame and split the dataset by wages into 5 bands:
  - 0 and Under 0
  - Over 0 and under 1000
  - 1000 to under 10000
  - 10000 and under 50000
  - 50000 and above

For those people who have **not** gone bankrupt (target=0) discover for each of the wage bands:
- % of people who own property
- % of people that have any type of CCJ
- % of People who have savings greater than 1000
- The average amount of savings for people who have over 1000 in savings

Export the results into Excel, create graphs and rename columns into suitably descriptive names.

7.5.3 Solution to exercise 7.2

Program 7-11: Exercise 7.2

```python
#import data – step1
sample = pd.read_csv("C:/temp/sample.csv")
# create a count column with a value 1 –step2
sample['count']=1
# replace na in certain columns with 0
sample['CCJ_government'] = sample['CCJ_government'].fillna(0)
sample['CCJ_private'] = sample['CCJ_private'].fillna(0)


# reduce the data frame to only include target equals 0 – step3
exer7_2 = sample[sample.target == 0 ]
#ccj flag for private or government – step4
exer7_2['ccj'] = np.where(exer7_2.CCJ_government>=1, 1,
              np.where(exer7_2.CCJ_private>=1, 1, 0))
#wage band -step5
exer7_2['wage_group'] = np.where(exer7_2.wages <=0, "0 and under 0",
             np.where(exer7_2.wages<1000, "0-1k",
             np.where(exer7_2.wages<10000, "1-10k",
             np.where(exer7_2.wages<50000, "10-50k",
             np.where(exer7_2.wages>=50000, "50k+", 'err'  )))))


#property – step6
exer7_2['property'] = np.where(exer7_2.properties>=1, 1, 0)


#savings over 1000 – step7
exer7_2['save1000'] = np.where(exer7_2.savings>=1000, 1, 0)
exer7_2['ovr1000'] = np.where(exer7_2.savings>=1000, exer7_2.savings, 0)


#always check your data to see if it works  Click on exer7_2 in the variable explorer pane
#summarising the data – step8
exer7_2b = exer7_2.groupby(['wage_group']).agg({'count':'sum','property':'sum','ccj':'sum',
             'save1000':'sum','ovr1000':'sum' }).reset_index()
```

1) Importing the data and quickly cleaning the NA values
2) creating our own count flag and replacing null value
3) To remove all bankruptcies
4) A command to give people 1 if they have 1 or more CCJ's
5) Creating our wage bands
6) A command to give people 1 if they have 1 or more properties
7) A command to give people 1 if they have savings over 1000 and creating a new column based on when savings is over 1000
8) Summarising the data

How you proceed next is a matter of choice, you can either calculate the figures in Python or export exer7_2b into Excel and calculate the figures in there.

Figure 7.7: Exercise 7.2 report in Excel

				Over 1000	
Wage Group	Count	% own property	% with CCJ	% with savings	Average savings amount
0 and under	51	29.4%	5.88%	5.9%	28857
0 to 1000	7449	12.8%	3.17%	1.0%	3111
1k to 10k	4541	20.0%	2.00%	12.5%	2462
10k to 50k	289	30.1%	1.38%	33.9%	4681
50k+	57	43.9%	1.75%	31.6%	13283

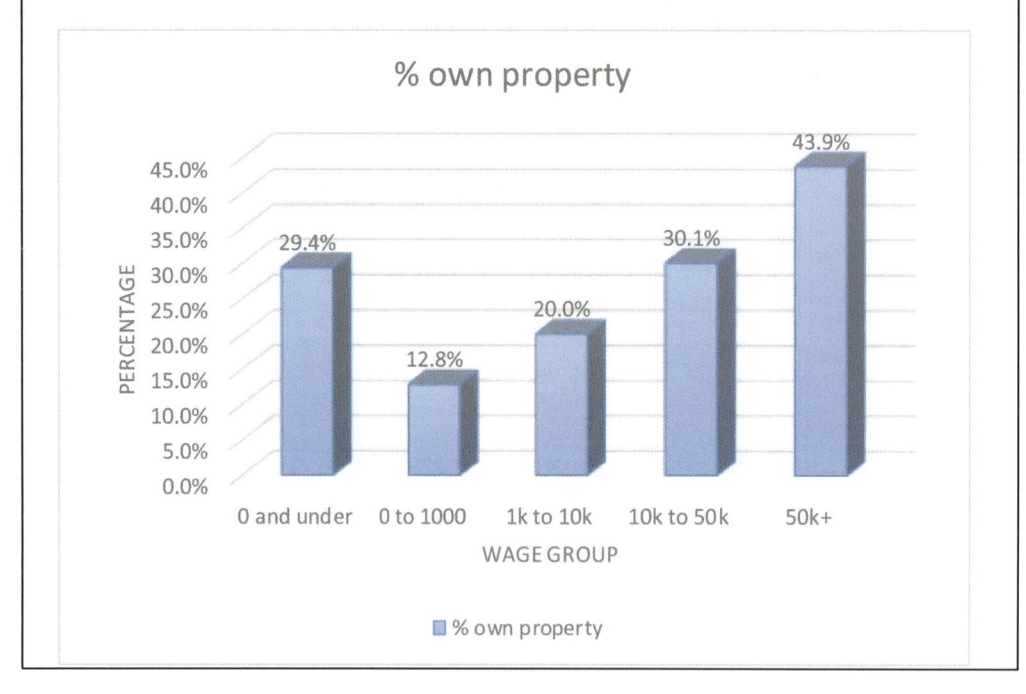

% own property

- 0 and under: 29.4%
- 0 to 1000: 12.8%
- 1k to 10k: 20.0%
- 10k to 50k: 30.1%
- 50k+: 43.9%

As mentioned previously, graphs and report tools are available in Python, but this book will use Excel, due to its simplicity and knowledge that managers tend to like their Excel graphs.

Excel commands used:
- % own property = property / count
- % with CCJ = CCJ / count
- % with savings over 1000 = save1000 / count
- Average savings amount = save1000 / ovr1000

7.6 Summary

Although we have covered much in this chapter, the new techniques introduced in this chapter is quite small.

The table below contains the key pieces of code as shown in the chapter

Table 7.4: Chapter 7 sample code

Sample Code	Description
exer7_2b = exer7_2.groupby(['wage_group']).agg({'count':'sum', 'property': 'sum','ccj':'sum','save1000': 'sum','ovr1000':'sum' }).reset_index()	Summarizes the data within a data frame by another variables
summar3['perc_privccj'] = round(summar3['ccj_priv'] / summar3['count'] ,4)	Creating a new column to create %, rounded to 4 decimal places
summar3.to_csv("C:/temp/summar3.csv", index = False)	Exporting a data frame into a CSV file

8. Simple linear regression in R

We covered simple linear regression in chapter 2, using Excel, and very briefly in chapter 4, using R.

This chapter will cover many of the aspects we have seen previously but in more detail.
The beginning of this chapter is different from the previous sections, as we focus slightly on the theory (in an applied manner).

This chapter will detail the calculation of specific statistics:
- Variance
- Standard deviation
- Standard error
- Simple linear regression
- R-squared

8.1 Introduction to regression

Linear regression has many practical uses. Most applications of linear regression fall into one of the following two broad categories:
- If the goal is prediction or forecasting, linear regression can be used to fit a predictive model to an observed data set of Y and X values.
- Attempt to model the relationship between two variables by fitting a linear equation to the observed data. For example, an analyst wants to find the relationship between the weight and height of individuals using a linear regression model.

8.1.1 Recap of simple linear regression

The aim of regression is to model the dependence of one variable Y on variable X.
- Y is called the *dependent* variable or the *response* variable.
- X is labelled as the *independent* variable, *covariate* or the *explanatory variable*.

The equation for a simple linear regression (as previously shown in section 1.5) is

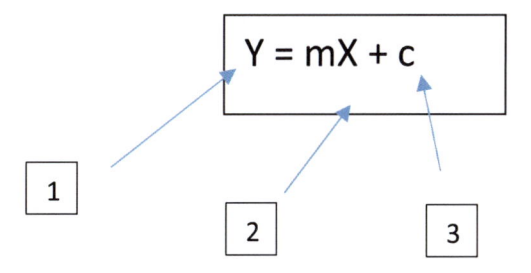

$$Y = mX + c$$

1
2
3

1) Is the dependent
2) Independent
3) The Intercept

The goal of linear regression is to find the line that best predicts Y from X

8.1.2 Normal distribution

The Normal or Gaussian distribution is the most important continuous distribution in Statistics.

Figure 8.1: Normal distribution

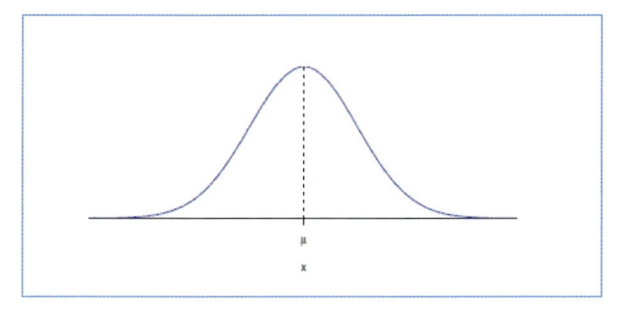

A plot of a normal distribution is a bell-shaped curve. The curve is symmetrical about the mean value so that the median and mode value is also its mean.

8.1.3 Calculating variance, standard deviation and standard error

Table 8.1: Mean, median, mode and range

	13, 18, 13, 14, 13, 16, 14, 21, 13	1, 2, 4, 7
Mean = the average of a group of numbers	15	3.5
Median = the middle number	14	3 (have to take middle of 3 and 4)
Mode = the number repeated most often	13	all numbers only appear once
Range = the full range of numbers	(21-13)=8	(7-1) =6

- **Variance (σ^2):** how much your observations vary from the mean e.g. numbers 1,2,4,7.

$$= \frac{\text{the sum of (each data point minus the mean)}^2}{\text{sample size}}$$

$$= \frac{(1-3.5)^2+(2-3.5)^2+(4-3.5)^2+(7-3.5)^2}{4 \; (number \; of \; observations)} = \frac{21}{4} = 5.25$$

- **Standard deviation(σ):** reflects both the deviation from the mean and the frequency of this deviation, using the above figures.

    Standard deviation (σ) = √ variance = √5.25 = 2.29

- **Standard error (SE):** another common measurement to describe the deviation from the mean and the frequency

$$\text{Standard error} = \sqrt{\frac{variance}{number \; of \; observations}} = \sqrt{\frac{5.25}{4}} = 1.14$$

8.1.4 Calculating simple linear regression

The simple linear regression has been covered previously. This section illustrates how to calculate this by hand and to provide a better understanding (if you are not interested then you can proceed to chapter 8.2).

> **Regression Formula:**
>
> Regression Equation (y) = c + mx
>
> Slope(m) = (NΣXY - (ΣX)(ΣY)) / (NΣX² - (ΣX)²)

Where:

- x and y are the variables.
- m is the slope of the regression line
- c is the intercept point of the regression line and the y-axis.
- N is the number of values or elements
- X is the first Score
- Y is the second Score
- ΣXY is the sum of the product of first and second Scores
- ΣX is the sum of First Scores
- ΣY is the sum of Second Scores
- ΣX² is the sum of square First Scores

8.1.5 Calculating the linear regression

Calculate the simple linear regression equation using the figures in table 8.2.

Table 8.2: Figures for calculating simple linear regression

X	Y
60	3.1
61	3.6
62	3.8
63	4
65	4.1

Solution to Example 8.1

Step 1:

Find N: as there are 5 figures, N=5

Step 2:

Calculate X*Y and X²

*Table 8.3: X*Y and X²*

X Value	Y Value	X*Y	X*X
60	3.1	60 * 3.1 = 186	60 * 60 = 3600
61	3.6	61 * 3.6 = 219.6	61 * 61 = 3721
62	3.8	62 * 3.8 = 235.6	62 * 62 = 3844
63	4	63 * 4 = 252	63 * 63 = 3969
65	4.1	65 * 4.1 = 266.5	65 * 65 = 4225

Step 3:

Find ΣX, ΣY, ΣXY, ΣX²

- ΣX = 60 + 61 + 62 + 63 + 65 = 311
- ΣY = 3.1 + 3.6 + 3.8 + 4 + 4.1 = 18.6
- ΣXY = 186 + 219.6 + 235.6 + 252 + 266.5 = 1159.7
- ΣX² = 3600 + 3721 + 3844 + 3969 + 4225 = 19539

Step 4

Substitute in the slope formula shown above

Slope(m) = (NΣXY - (ΣX)(ΣY)) / (NΣX² - (ΣX)²)

= ((5)*(1159.7)-(311)*(18.6)) / ((5)*(19359)-(311)²)

= (5798.5 - 5784.6) / (96795 - 96721)

= 13.9 / 74

= 0.19

Step 5

Substitute in the intercept formula given

Intercept(c) = (ΣY - b(ΣX)) / N

= (18.6 - 0.19(311)) / 5

= (18.6 - 59.09) / 5

= -40.49 / 5

= -8.098

Step 6

Substitute these values in regression equation formula

Regression Equation y = mx + c

= 0.19x -8.098

Suppose if we want to know the value of y when the variable x = 64. Then we can substitute the value in the equation previously derived.

> Regression Equation (y) = a + bx
> $\qquad$ = -8.098 + 0.19(64).
> $\qquad$ = -8.098 + 12.16
> $\qquad$ = 4.06

So when x=64, we should expect y to equal 4.06

8.1.6 Calculating R-squared

r^2: a measure of goodness-of-fit of linear regression.

The value r^2 is a fraction between 0.0 and 1.0 and has no units. An r^2 value of 0.0 means that knowing X does not help you predict Y. There is no linear relationship between X and Y, and the best-fit line is a horizontal line going through the mean of all Y values. When r^2 equals 1.0, all points lie exactly on a straight line with no scatter. Knowing X lets you predict Y perfectly. An R-square value over 0.7 signifies a good fit.

8.1.7 Example of calculating the r-square

A statistical measure of how well a regression line approximates real data points. The formula for r-squared is:

$$1 - \frac{the\ sum\ of\ squared\ distances\ between\ the\ predicted\ and\ actual\ values\ of\ Y}{sum\ of\ squared\ distances\ between\ the\ mean\ of\ Y\ and\ their\ actual\ value}$$

Table 8.4: Calculating key figures for r-squared

X	y	Predicted Y	Error (Y-predicted Y)	Error squared	the distance between Y values and mean	mean distance squared
60	3.1	3.302	-0.202	0.040804	0.62	0.3844
61	3.6	3.492	0.108	0.011664	0.12	0.0144
62	3.8	3.682	0.118	0.013924	-0.08	0.0064
63	4	3.872	0.128	0.016384	-0.28	0.0784
65	4.1	4.252	-0.152	0.023104	-0.38	0.1444
mean	3.72		sum	0.10588	sum	0.628

$$= 1 - \frac{0.10588}{0.628} = 0.831$$

With a high r-square value, we know that we can use the model produced with confidence.

8.2 Python calculating simple linear regression

Program 8-1: Simple linear regression

```
#import libraries
import numpy as np
import pandas as pd

#linear regression
from sklearn.linear_model import LinearRegression
x = np.array([60, 61, 62,63, 65]).reshape((-1, 1))
y = np.array([3.1, 3.6, 3.8, 4 ,4.1])

model = LinearRegression()
model.fit(x, y)
intercept=model.intercept_
coef =  model.coef_
r_sq = model.score(x, y)
print(intercept)
print(coef)
print(r_sq)
```

Figure 8.2: Python simple linear regression results

```
In [2]: print(intercept)
   ...: print(coef)
   ...: print(r_sq)
-7.96351351351351
[0.18783784]
0.831511447753486
```

Regression Equation y = mx + c

From figure 8.2 it can be observed that:

- C = -7.96351
- M = 0.18784

Regression Equation y = 0.18784x – 7.96351

8.3 Exercise in Python- simple linear regression

8.3.1 Linear regression scenario

In the sale of new cars, it is generally the case that the more expensive the car, the greater the profit to the dealer. The sales manager wants to help the company's salespersons to make the most profitable sales possible to each customer. One particular area of interest concerns the amount of credit successfully applied for new car purchases. The manager has obtained a sample of 30 recently completed car sales where the customer secured a credit loan. A CSV file called **reg01** contains two variables:

- X: the gross annual income of the purchasers (in 1,000s)
- Y: the amount of credit loan obtained by the purchaser (in 1,000s)

It would be clearly helpful for a salesperson to know how much credit a potential purchaser can be persuaded to apply for, given the knowledge of their income.

In this example, we will be using a different library for our regression, as it provides more statistics in its results.

8.3.2 Python linear regression solution

Program 8-2: Simple linear regression – Exercise

```
#8.3.1 Linear regression scenario – step 1
import statsmodels.api as sm

#import data
reg01 = pd.read_csv("C:/temp/reg01.csv")

#create our target –step2
y = reg01['Y']

#create our variables –step3
x = reg01['X']
#need to create a constant for the intercept
x = sm.add_constant(x)

#the model –step4
model = sm.OLS(y, x)

#the results –step5
results = model.fit()
#print our results – step6
print(results.summary())
```

1) First, we need to activate a new library and import the data
2) **y = reg01['Y']** - from our data frame reg01, we need to create a **series** (an array) with just our target variables, **y**
3) Next stage involves creating a data with the variable we want t use to predict **y**. The package **statmodel** in Python does not include an intercept in its results, unless a variable has been created. In this case, we have used **sm.add_constant(x)**. The same result can be achieved with **x['const'] = 1.**

4) The model is based on ordinary least squares (OLS), where use everything that is in the data frame **x**, to predict **y.**
5) By calling .fit(), we obtain the variable results. This object holds a lot of information about the regression model.
6) Prints our full results, as shown in figure 8.3

Figure 8.3: Simple linear regression results

```
                            OLS Regression Results
==============================================================================
Dep. Variable:                      Y   R-squared:                       0.768
Model:                            OLS   Adj. R-squared:                  0.760
Method:                 Least Squares   F-statistic:                     92.91
Date:                Tue, 28 Apr 2020   Prob (F-statistic):           2.15e-10
Time:                        13:00:22   Log-Likelihood:                -53.604
No. Observations:                  30   AIC:                             111.2
Df Residuals:                      28   BIC:                             114.0
Df Model:                           1
Covariance Type:            nonrobust
==============================================================================
                 coef    std err          t      P>|t|      [0.025      0.975]
------------------------------------------------------------------------------
const          3.4363      0.675      5.091      0.000       2.054       4.819
X              0.1956      0.020      9.639      0.000       0.154       0.237
==============================================================================
Omnibus:                        0.147   Durbin-Watson:                   1.896
Prob(Omnibus):                  0.929   Jarque-Bera (JB):                0.094
Skew:                           0.106   Prob(JB):                        0.954
Kurtosis:                       2.827   Cond. No.                         82.3
==============================================================================
```

A brief description of some of results is described below:

- **R-Square** - R-Squared is the proportion of variance in the dependent variable which can be explained by the independent variables. R-square is the statistic to measure how well the model is fitting the actual data, which had been calculated earlier.
- **Adjusted R-Squared** - In multiple regression models, the r-squared will increase as more variables are included in the model. This is an adjustment of the R-squared that penalizes the addition of extraneous predictors to the model. Adjusted R-squared is computed using the formula 1 - ((1 - Rsq)(N - 1) /(N - k - 1)) where k is the number of predictors.
- **F-Statistic** - the Mean Square Model divided by the Mean Square Error. This is a good indicator of whether there is a relationship between the predictor and the response variables. The further the F-statistic is from 1 the better it is.
- **coef** – our model values, which was manually calculated previously.

- **Std. Error** – measures the average amount that the coefficient estimates vary from the actual average value of our response variable. We'd ideally want a lower number relative to its coefficients
- **T value** - this is a measure of how many standard deviations our coefficient estimate is far away from 0. For the t-value, the higher the number the stronger at predicting the variable is. Additionally, t-values are also used to compute p-values.
- **Pr|>t|** tells us the strength of predicting 'y'. The lower the value the stronger the variable. A p-value of 0.05 (5%) or less is a good cut-off point.
-

Applying **y=mx + c.**

> Predicted credit = 3.4363 + 0.1956*salary

With a positive value on the parameter estimate, we can deduce that as salary increases, so does the loan amount. Additionally, with an r-square greater than 0.7 (0.7684), we can use these results with confidence.

Therefore, for those people with a salary of 10,000, we can predict that their loan availability would be

$$3.43 + (0.19558 * 10)$$
$$3.43 + 1.9558$$
$$5.1858$$

Therefore, predict credit = 5185.80. The variable salary's units were in the 1000s, therefore we had to make the necessary calculations to produce the predicted credit amount accurately.

8.4 Summary

The main aim of this chapters was to lay the foundations for linear regression and its application. I have experienced many people who say that they understand linear regression, but fail to grasp the basics that this chapter covers.

9 Multiple linear regression

It is a rare occurrence when we can use only one variable to predict an outcome with confidence. When we use more than one explanatory variable to predict the outcome (Y), we call this multiple linear regression.

This chapter covers the topics:
- Multiple linear regression
- Creating an output file
- Sequential elimination approaches
- Modelling categorical variables

On a personal note, this is when linear regression becomes interesting and more demanding (possibly more fun).

9.1 Multiple linear regression

Previously we have only considered one explanatory variable. Multiple linear regression uses more than one explanatory variable to produce our linear equation.

$$Y = c + M_1 x_1 + M_2 x_2 + \cdots + M_p x_p + \varepsilon$$

1. 2. 3. 4.

1) The dependent (y)
2) The intercept (c)
3) The independents / explanatory variables
4) The error term
   a. When developing models, the error term value is very close to zero, so is ignored. This is only here for equation accuracy and won't be considered further on

Sometimes, you may see the equation written as

$$Y = \beta_0 + \beta_1 X_1 + \beta_2 X_2 + \cdots + \beta_n X_n + \varepsilon$$

As you can see, we are only replacing M with β, so it is about choice and style.

9.1.1 Example of multiple linear regression

A CSV file called **multi1** contains values of the following variables for a sample of 19 companies

- Company – the name of the company
- Profit – company's profit margin %
- Growth - company's growth rate
- PER – company's price-earnings (P-E) ratio

Our first example involves constructing a multiple linear regression model to predict PER from profit and growth.

Solution is on next page

Program 9-1: Example 9-1 Multi linear regression

```python
import numpy as np
import pandas as pd

#9.1.1 Linear regression scenario
import statsmodels.api as sm

#import data
multi1 = pd.read_csv("C:/temp/multi1.csv")

#create our target
y = multi1['PER']

# our variables
x = multi1[['Growth', 'Profit']]
# add constant
x = sm.add_constant(x)

#create model
model = sm.OLS(y, x)

#get results for model
results = model.fit()
print(results.summary())
```

The program is very similar to program 8-2, with the only difference, is that our **x** data frame has 2 variables

Figure 9.1: Multiple linear regression results

```
                            OLS Regression Results
==============================================================================
Dep. Variable:                    PER   R-squared:                       0.591
Model:                            OLS   Adj. R-squared:                  0.540
Method:                 Least Squares   F-statistic:                     11.57
Date:                Tue, 28 Apr 2020   Prob (F-statistic):           0.000779
Time:                        13:29:48   Log-Likelihood:                -42.731
No. Observations:                  19   AIC:                             91.46
Df Residuals:                      16   BIC:                             94.30
Df Model:                           2
Covariance Type:            nonrobust
==============================================================================
                 coef    std err          t      P>|t|      [0.025      0.975]
------------------------------------------------------------------------------
const          5.5598      1.600      3.474      0.003       2.167       8.952
Growth         0.2038      0.140      1.453      0.165      -0.093       0.501
Profit         0.4654      0.143      3.252      0.005       0.162       0.769
==============================================================================
Omnibus:                        0.122   Durbin-Watson:                   1.572
Prob(Omnibus):                  0.941   Jarque-Bera (JB):                0.345
Skew:                           0.039   Prob(JB):                        0.842
Kurtosis:                       2.345   Cond. No.                         44.6
==============================================================================
```

Using the estimates, the multiple linear regression is:

Predicted PER = 5.56 + (0.47 * Profit) + (0.20 * Growth)

As this equation uses two explanatory variables, we have to use the adjusted r-square for its performance. With an adjusted r-square of 0.54, we may not consider using this model as it falls under the 0.7 mark, but if we lack an alternative model then we would have to use it.

Note: even though we can make statistical models, sometimes the model is not accurate to enough to use with confidence. As usual, there is an exception to the rule, some managers would prefer a weak model rather than no model. As an analyst, we just provide as much information as possible for the managers to make the decisions.

9.2 Creating a scored output file

Sometimes, the results are not enough and we want the predicted values on a data frame. Within Python we can create an output file with the predicted values, without the need to score the data frame ourselves. You can obtain the predicted values by using .fittedvalues

Program 9-2: Obtaining predicted value

```
multi1['predy'] = results.fittedvalues
```

Figure 9.2: The output file with the predicted result

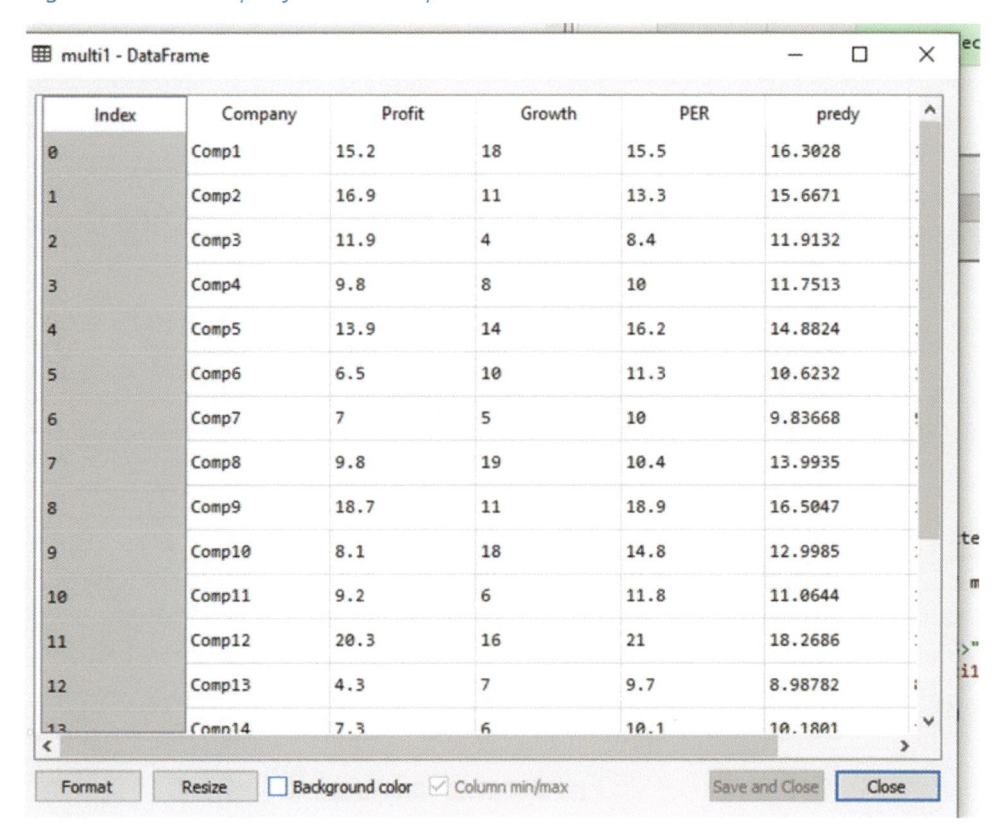

Index	Company	Profit	Growth	PER	predy
0	Comp1	15.2	18	15.5	16.3028
1	Comp2	16.9	11	13.3	15.6671
2	Comp3	11.9	4	8.4	11.9132
3	Comp4	9.8	8	10	11.7513
4	Comp5	13.9	14	16.2	14.8824
5	Comp6	6.5	10	11.3	10.6232
6	Comp7	7	5	10	9.83668
7	Comp8	9.8	19	10.4	13.9935
8	Comp9	18.7	11	18.9	16.5047
9	Comp10	8.1	18	14.8	12.9985
10	Comp11	9.2	6	11.8	11.0644
11	Comp12	20.3	16	21	18.2686
12	Comp13	4.3	7	9.7	8.98782
13	Comp14	7.3	6	10.1	10.1801

You have now created a data frame with the predicted values.

Exercise 9.1

A CSV file multi2 contains the first order of drinks consumed in a restaurant/bar based on first 31 days.
- Day – the day of the month
- x1 - Average price of a drink
- x2 – Drinks ordered
- x3 - Average daytime temperature (F)
- Y – drinks remaining (pint)

Construct a multiple linear regression model to predict Y from x1, x2 and x3. Also, add to the data frame, multi2, the predicted values in a column.

Is the model predictive?

Solution to exercise 9.1

Program 9-3: Exercise 9.1 Multi linear regression

```
#import data
multi2 = pd.read_csv("C:/temp/multi2.csv")


#create our target
y = multi2['Y']


# our variables
x = multi2[['X1', 'X2', 'X3']]
# add constant
x = sm.add_constant(x)


#create model
model = sm.OLS(y, x)


#get results for model
results = model.fit()
print(results.summary())


#predicted y
multi2['predcted_y'] = results.fittedvalues
```

Figure 9.3: Solution to Exercise 9.1

```
...: print(results.summary())
                            OLS Regression Results
==============================================================================
Dep. Variable:                      Y   R-squared:                       0.713
Model:                            OLS   Adj. R-squared:                  0.681
Method:                 Least Squares   F-statistic:                     22.32
Date:                Tue, 28 Apr 2020   Prob (F-statistic):           1.78e-07
Time:                        14:04:26   Log-Likelihood:                -10.730
No. Observations:                  31   AIC:                             29.46
Df Residuals:                      27   BIC:                             35.20
Df Model:                           3
Covariance Type:            nonrobust
==============================================================================
                 coef    std err          t      P>|t|      [0.025      0.975]
------------------------------------------------------------------------------
const          2.1336      2.687      0.794      0.434     -3.380       7.647
X1            -1.0212      0.789     -1.294      0.207     -2.640       0.598
X2             0.2161      0.078      2.781      0.010      0.057       0.375
X3             0.0338      0.004      7.798      0.000      0.025       0.043
==============================================================================
Omnibus:                        0.686   Durbin-Watson:                   2.121
Prob(Omnibus):                  0.710   Jarque-Bera (JB):                0.143
Skew:                           0.140   Prob(JB):                        0.931
Kurtosis:                       3.179   Cond. No.                     2.27e+03
==============================================================================
```

Multi-linear equation is:

$$Predicted\ drink\ remaining = 2.134 - (1.021 * X1) + (0.216 * X2) + (0.034 * X3)$$

As this model has 3 explanatory variables, we use the adjusted r-square value, which is 0.6807. With a value close to 0.7, we can consider using this model with confidence.

The 0.7 cut-off can be considered as a guide and not as an absolute rule.

9.3 The t-statistic

The t-statistic was briefly covered in chapter 8.

If we view the results from exercise 9.1 (figure 9.3), we will notice t-values and the t-statistic.

The t-statistic provides information regarding how significant the variable is, to the model.

Table 9.1: T-statistic significance rating

Value	Significance level	Strength of Variable
>0.05	Not significant	Insufficient
0.01<0.05	0.05 or 5%	Significant
0.001<0.01	0.01 or 1%	Strong
<0.001	0.001 or 0.1%	Very strong

These statistics are very important, as it tells us which variables should be considered within the model.

Example 9.3

Using the previous results of drinks remaining, which variable does not contribute significantly to the model?

Figure 9.4: T-statistics for drink

```
               coef    std err       t      P>|t|    [0.025    0.975]
-----------------------------------------------------------------------
const        2.1336    2.687      0.794    0.434    -3.380     7.647
X1          -1.0212    0.789     -1.294    0.207    -2.640     0.598
X2           0.2161    0.078      2.781    0.010     0.057     0.375
X3           0.0338    0.004      7.798    0.000     0.025     0.043
=======================================================================
```

1) The t-statistics are labelled Pr(>|t|

From Figure 9.4, X1 average price of drink per pint does not contribute (we ignore the intercept).

In this scenario, it would be recommended to re-run the model excluding the explanatory variable 'X1', as shown in program 9-4.

Program 9-4: Exercise 9.1 Multi linear regression without X1

```
#import data
multi2 = pd.read_csv("C:/temp/multi2.csv")


#create our target
y = multi2['Y']


# our variables
x = multi2[[ 'X2', 'X3']]
# add constant
x = sm.add_constant(x)


#create model
model = sm.OLS(y, x)


#get results for model
results = model.fit()
print(results.summary())
```

Figure 9.5: New solution for predicting drinks remaining

```
                            OLS Regression Results
==============================================================================
Dep. Variable:                      Y   R-squared:                       0.695
Model:                            OLS   Adj. R-squared:                  0.673
Method:                 Least Squares   F-statistic:                     31.87
Date:                Tue, 28 Apr 2020   Prob (F-statistic):           6.09e-08
Time:                        14:25:00   Log-Likelihood:                -11.663
No. Observations:                  31   AIC:                             29.33
Df Residuals:                      28   BIC:                             33.63
Df Model:                           2
Covariance Type:            nonrobust
==============================================================================
                 coef    std err          t      P>|t|      [0.025      0.975]
------------------------------------------------------------------------------
const         -1.0599      1.076     -0.985      0.333     -3.264       1.144
X2             0.2319      0.078      2.987      0.006      0.073       0.391
X3             0.0346      0.004      7.971      0.000      0.026       0.044
==============================================================================
Omnibus:                        2.992   Durbin-Watson:                   2.268
Prob(Omnibus):                  0.224   Jarque-Bera (JB):                1.674
Skew:                           0.487   Prob(JB):                        0.433
Kurtosis:                       3.589   Cond. No.                         868.
==============================================================================
```

1) With the explanatory variables having a t-statistic of less than 0.05, the explanatory variables can be used with confidence.
2) The r-square and adjusted r-square have not reduced significantly

Note that the parameter estimates and the intercept values have changed, which means that we have a new multi-linear model.

$$Predicted\ drinks\ remaining = -1.06 + (0.232 * X2) + (0.0.35 * X3)$$

We have conducted a sequential approach called backwards elimination, by removing a weak performing variable.

Variable selection techniques tend to cause arguments among data scientists/statisticians, which I will not go into here. There are always people dismissing procedures, no matter what field you are in. I only mention this so that you are aware of this argument.

9.4 Exercise 9.2

A CSV file called multi3 contains monthly teaching hours for schools split by districts. The file contains the following columns:

- Pupils – average pupils in school
- Books – books in school
- Teachinghrs – teaching hours
- Population – population in the district (000s)
- Absentrate – pupil absent rate
- pupilhours – hours pupils are in school

Create a mode to Predict teaching hours only using the variables are predictive (p>|t|) below 0.05)

Hint: model all of the variables first, then reduce one variable at a time

Program 9-5: Exercise 9.2 part1

```
#import data
multi3 = pd.read_csv("C:/temp/multi3.csv")


#create our target
y = multi3['teachinghrs']


# our variables
x = multi3[['pupils', 'books', 'population', 'absentrate', 'pupilhours' ]]
# add constant
x = sm.add_constant(x)


#create model
model = sm.OLS(y, x)


#get results for model
results = model.fit()
print(results.summary())
```

Figure 9.6: Exercise 9.2 part1 results

```
==============================================================================
                coef    std err          t      P>|t|      [0.025      0.975]
------------------------------------------------------------------------------
const        101.5002    126.042      0.805      0.438    -175.917     378.917
pupils        22.7595      0.807     28.196      0.000      20.983      24.536
books         -0.0004      0.004     -0.109      0.915      -0.008       0.008
population    -1.1436      0.459     -2.492      0.030      -2.153      -0.134
absentrate   -27.4447     27.463     -0.999      0.339     -87.891      33.002
pupilhours     0.0146      0.030      0.494      0.631      -0.051       0.080
==============================================================================
```

With books having a p>|t| 0f 0.915, this will be the first variable to go.

Program 9-6: Exercise 9.2 part2

```
#y has already been defined
# our variables
x = multi3[['pupils', 'population', 'absentrate', 'pupilhours' ]]
# add constant
x = sm.add_constant(x)


#create model
model = sm.OLS(y, x)


#get results for model
results = model.fit()
print(results.summary())
```

Figure 9.7: Exercise 9.2 part2 results

```
==============================================================================
                coef    std err          t      P>|t|      [0.025      0.975]
------------------------------------------------------------------------------
const        103.1989    119.817      0.861      0.406    -157.859     364.257
pupils        22.7939      0.712     32.019      0.000      21.243      24.345
population    -1.1592      0.418     -2.775      0.017      -2.069      -0.249
absentrate   -27.8304     26.090     -1.067      0.307     -84.675      29.014
pupilhours     0.0126      0.022      0.570      0.579      -0.036       0.061
==============================================================================
```

With pupilhours having a p>|t| 0f 0.579, this will be the next variable to go.

Program 9-7: Exercise 9.2 part3

```
#y has already been defined
# our variables
x = multi3[['pupils', 'population', 'absentrate' ]]
# add constant
x = sm.add_constant(x)


#create model
model = sm.OLS(y, x)


#get results for model
results = model.fit()
print(results.summary())
```

Figure 9.8: Exercise 9.2 part 3 results

```
==============================================================================
                 coef    std err          t      P>|t|      [0.025      0.975]
------------------------------------------------------------------------------
const        144.7308     92.603      1.563      0.142     -55.326     344.787
pupils        23.1635      0.286     81.035      0.000      22.546      23.781
population    -1.2056      0.399     -3.023      0.010      -2.067      -0.344
absentrate   -37.3370     19.532     -1.912      0.078     -79.533       4.859
==============================================================================
```

With absentrate having a p>|t| 0f 0.078, this will be the next variable to go.

Program 9-8: Exercise 9.2 part4

```
#y has already been defined
# our variables
x = multi3[['pupils', 'population']]
# add constant
x = sm.add_constant(x)


#create model
model = sm.OLS(y, x)


#get results for model
results = model.fit()
print(results.summary())
```

Figure 9.9: Exercise 9.2 part 4 results

```
Dep. Variable:             teachinghrs   R-squared:                    1.000
Model:                             OLS   Adj. R-squared:               1.000
Method:                  Least Squares   F-statistic:              4.871e+04
Date:                 Tue, 28 Apr 2020   Prob (F-statistic):        1.26e-27
Time:                         15:49:47   Log-Likelihood:             -94.492
No. Observations:                   17   AIC:                          195.0
Df Residuals:                       14   BIC:                          197.5
Df Model:                            2
Covariance Type:             nonrobust
==============================================================================
                 coef    std err          t      P>|t|      [0.025      0.975]
------------------------------------------------------------------------------
const        -27.2575     23.904     -1.140      0.273     -78.527      24.012
pupils        22.7485      0.203    112.145      0.000      22.313      23.184
population    -0.7273      0.339     -2.147      0.050      -1.454      -0.001
==============================================================================
Omnibus:                        8.463   Durbin-Watson:                   1.749
Prob(Omnibus):                  0.015   Jarque-Bera (JB):                5.826
Skew:                          -1.397   Prob(JB):                       0.0543
Kurtosis:                       3.649   Cond. No.                         538.
==============================================================================
```

Teachinghrs = -27.258 + 22.75*pupils – 0.727*population

With an Adj- R-squared of 1 being recorded at each iteration, this could be a cause of concern. Any model that has an adjusted R-square value greater than 0.95 would need investigating as, most probably, one of the independent variables is an almost copy of the dependent variable.

9.5 Categorical variables in the model

When dealing with regression, occasionally we use categorical variables, as well as continuous variables. The solution is quite straightforward; we create dummy variables.

9.5.1 Creating the dummy variables

Dummy variables are independent variables which take the value of either 0 or 1. As an example, if we had a variable called children which had two values, yes and no. Creating dummy values of this variable requires:

Create two new columns
- Children_y
    - Where children ='Y' makes this column equal 1 else make it equal 0
- Children_n
    - Where children ='N' makes this column equal 1 else make it equal 0

So, in essence, for every bin created, we create that number of columns based on each value.

9.5.2 Dummy variable trap

When creating the dummy variables, we need to cautious of using all of the dummy variables created. For every categorical variable, with *k* number of bins, we only need *k-1* dummy variables. If we include all dummy variables, then the model will suffer from multicollinearity (the dummy variable trap), as they will be highly correlated (one can be predicted from the other). Using our children variable example, for every time children_y =1, children_n =0 and vice versa. Therefore, we could use children_y to predict children _n

To solve this issue, when we create our model, we exclude one of the dummy variables from each variable we wish to model, e.g., for children we could only include children_y. The dummy variable dropped is given a score of 0.

9.5.3 Example of categorical regression

Categorical variables can provide further insight into predicting outcomes, e.g. customer gender, region or sometimes we may want to group continuous variables into groups, e.g. age.

A CSV file called **categ1** contains 19 companies with the following variables:

- company – company name
- Profit – company's profit margin %
- Growth - company's growth rate
- PER – company's price-earnings (P-E) ratio
- Industry - Industry has 3 categories:
    - 1= Financial
    - 2= Utilities
    - 3 = Computing

Import this data and construct a multiple linear regression model to predict PER from profit, growth and industry.

Solution is on next page

Program 9-9: Exercise 9.3 part1

```python
#import data
categ1 = pd.read_csv("C:/temp/categ1.csv")


# create our dummy variables

categ1['industy_1'] = np.where(categ1.Industry==1, 1, 0)
categ1['industy_2'] = np.where(categ1.Industry==2, 1, 0)
categ1['industy_3'] = np.where(categ1.Industry==3, 1, 0)


# will use industry1 as our 0 variable
#create our target
y = categ1['PER']


# our variables
x = categ1[['Profit', 'Growth', 'industy_2', 'industy_3']]
# add constant
x = sm.add_constant(x)


#create model
model = sm.OLS(y, x)


#get results for model
results = model.fit()
print(results.summary())
```

Figure 9.10: Exercise 9.3 part1

```
                            OLS Regression Results
==============================================================================
Dep. Variable:                    PER   R-squared:                       0.695
Model:                            OLS   Adj. R-squared:                  0.608
Method:                 Least Squares   F-statistic:                     7.965
Date:                Tue, 28 Apr 2020   Prob (F-statistic):            0.00145
Time:                        16:12:46   Log-Likelihood:                -44.944
No. Observations:                  19   AIC:                             99.89
Df Residuals:                      14   BIC:                             104.6
Df Model:                           4
Covariance Type:            nonrobust
==============================================================================
                 coef    std err          t      P>|t|      [0.025      0.975]
------------------------------------------------------------------------------
const         10.0777      2.207      4.567      0.000       5.345      14.811
Profit         0.1979      0.227      0.873      0.397      -0.288       0.684
Growth         0.2766      0.170      1.623      0.127      -0.089       0.642
industy_2      3.8794      2.900      1.338      0.202      -2.341      10.100
industy_3     -1.0858      1.962     -0.553      0.589      -5.294       3.122
==============================================================================
```

1) With a categorical variable included each bin has been given its own score
    a. Industry 1 (missing from the results) has a value of 0.
    b. Unlike with continuous variables, where we multiple the explanatory variable by the estimates, for categorical they just have a fixed value

2) The results gathered has shown us that Profit is not a good explanatory variable to predict PER

So we need to model again, excluding Profit.

Program 9-10: Exercise 9.3 part2

```
#dummy variable and target already defined
# our variables
x = categ1[['Growth', 'industy_2', 'industy_3']]
# add constant
x = sm.add_constant(x)


#create model
model = sm.OLS(y, x)


#get results for model
results = model.fit()
print(results.summary())
```

Figure 9.11: Exercise 9.3 part1

```
                            OLS Regression Results
==============================================================================
Dep. Variable:                    PER   R-squared:                       0.678
Model:                            OLS   Adj. R-squared:                  0.614
Method:                 Least Squares   F-statistic:                     10.53
Date:                Tue, 28 Apr 2020   Prob (F-statistic):           0.000557
Time:                        16:19:49   Log-Likelihood:                -45.448
No. Observations:                  19   AIC:                             98.90
Df Residuals:                      15   BIC:                             102.7
Df Model:                           3
Covariance Type:            nonrobust
==============================================================================
                 coef    std err          t      P>|t|      [0.025      0.975]
------------------------------------------------------------------------------
const         11.3411      1.653      6.860      0.000       7.817      14.865
Growth         0.3155      0.163      1.932      0.072      -0.033       0.663
industy_2      5.7728      1.911      3.021      0.009       1.699       9.846
industy_3     -0.5862      1.862     -0.315      0.757      -4.554       3.382
```

From the recent results, industry_3 is not predictive, therefore we must drop this, combine with industry_1. This was removed at last stage, as some analysts would include this in their model, as it is part of a variable. As always, the choice is yours.

Program 9-11: Exercise 9.3 part3

```
#dummy variable and target already defined
x = categ1[['Growth', 'industy_2']]
# add constant
x = sm.add_constant(x)


#create model
model = sm.OLS(y, x)


#get results for model
results = model.fit()
print(results.summary())
```

Figure 9.12: Exercise 9.3 part1

```
Dep. Variable:                  PER   R-squared:                       0.676
Model:                          OLS   Adj. R-squared:                  0.635
Method:               Least Squares   F-statistic:                     16.69
Date:              Tue, 28 Apr 2020   Prob (F-statistic):           0.000122
Time:                      16:27:14   Log-Likelihood:                 -45.511
No. Observations:                19   AIC:                             97.02
Df Residuals:                    16   BIC:                             99.85
Df Model:                         2
Covariance Type:          nonrobust
==============================================================================
                 coef    std err          t      P>|t|      [0.025      0.975]
------------------------------------------------------------------------------
const         11.1177      1.451      7.664      0.000       8.042      14.193
Growth         0.3027      0.154      1.970      0.066      -0.023       0.628
industy_2      6.1414      1.467      4.185      0.001       3.031       9.252
------------------------------------------------------------------------------
```

Growth has pr(>|t|) value greater than 0.05, so we may want to remove this variable manually, this is a personal choice. In this instance, we are not and will just write up the final results

- For Industry 1 and 3: 11.1177 + 0 + (0.3027 * Growth)
- For Industry 2: 11.177+ 6.1414 + (0.3027 * Growth)

Throughout this exercise the Adj-R-squared, moved from 0.695 to 0.676. This shows that dropping weak variables does not overly impact the performance of the model.

Summary

Creating regression models is straightforward. Hopefully, you have noticed that the steps were as follows:

1) Import data
2) Define our target
3) Define our variables
4) Create model
5) Check variables were predictive, if not go back to 3, until complete
6) Ensure model is strong enough to predict (adj. R-squared)

The main concern when creating models is always the data. Without a true understanding of the data, the model you create could produce unrealistic results with strange variables.

10 Logistic regression

Logistic regression is used to calculate the probability of an event occurring, e.g. person responding to a direct mail campaign or a customer going bankrupt. When considering a logistic regression, we add up the model scores, then convert it into a probability, as will be demonstrated.

10.1 Logistic explanation

The logit is a device for constraining the probability between 0 and 1

$$\text{logit}(p_i) = \ln\left(\frac{p_i}{1-p_i}\right) = z \Leftrightarrow p_i = \left(\frac{1}{1+e^{-z}}\right)$$

- *Where z is the linear combination which can take any value*

Figure 10.1: Logistic graph plot

From figure 10.1, it can be clearly seen that the model shape is no longer linear and is more similar to that of an s-shape.

10.2 Logistic model

10.2.1 Creating a logistic model

Python fits linear logistic regression models for a binary outcome (for example, success or failure). The approach is similar to chapter 9:
- Import data
- Activate libraries
- Define our target variables
- Define our predictor variables
    - Create dummy variables if necessary
- Create model
- Decipher results

10.2.2 Example of creating a logistic model

This example uses a CSV file called logistic1, import this file and call the data frame logistic1. This file has a binary response variable called **sold**, which is equal to 1 if a sale has been made, and 0 otherwise. There are three predictor variables:
- Income (continuous)
- Mortgage % (% of wages go toward mortgage) (continuous)
- Tier (customer rank) (categorical/discrete).

The variable **tier** takes on the values 1 to 4. Tiers with a rank of 1 have the highest prestige, while those with 4 have the lowest.

Solution

Program 10-1: First logistic model

```python
import numpy as np
import pandas as pd

#import data
logistic1 = pd.read_csv("C:/temp/logistic1.csv")

#create our target
y = logistic1['sold']

#create dummy variables
logistic1['tier_1'] = np.where(logistic1.tier==1, 1, 0)
logistic1['tier_2'] = np.where(logistic1.tier==2, 1, 0)
logistic1['tier_3'] = np.where(logistic1.tier==3, 1, 0)
logistic1['tier_4'] = np.where(logistic1.tier==4, 1, 0)

# our predictor variables
x = logistic1[['income', 'mortgage', 'tier_2', 'tier_3', 'tier_4' ]]
# add constant
x['const'] = 1

# call the library
import statsmodels.api as sm

#the model code
logit_model=sm.Logit(y,x)

# get the results for the mode

result=logit_model.fit()
print(result.summary())
```

As we can see the code looks very similar to chapter 9 (program 9-11), where the only main difference is that

1. instead of using **OLS**, we are using **Logit**

Figure 10.2: Python logistic output

```
In [13]: print(result.summary())
                           Logit Regression Results
==============================================================================
Dep. Variable:                   sold   No. Observations:                  400
Model:                          Logit   Df Residuals:                      394
Method:                           MLE   Df Model:                            5
Date:                Thu, 30 Apr 2020   Pseudo R-squ.:                  0.08292
Time:                        08:21:09   Log-Likelihood:                -229.26
converged:                       True   LL-Null:                       -249.99
Covariance Type:            nonrobust   LLR p-value:                 7.578e-08
==============================================================================
                 coef    std err          z      P>|z|      [0.025      0.975]
------------------------------------------------------------------------------
income         0.0002      0.000      2.070      0.038     1.2e-05       0.000
mortgage       0.0804      0.033      2.423      0.015       0.015       0.145
tier_2        -0.6754      0.316     -2.134      0.033      -1.296      -0.055
tier_3        -1.3402      0.345     -3.881      0.000      -2.017      -0.663
tier_4        -1.5515      0.418     -3.713      0.000      -2.370      -0.733
const         -3.9900      1.140     -3.500      0.000      -6.224      -1.756
==============================================================================
```

We can treat 'P>|z|' values as we did previously with P>|t|. As we can see, all variables satisfy the 0.05 rule.

Our equation here is:

- Score = -3.99 + (income * 0.0002) + (mortgage*0.0804) + (Tier estimate)

But, we have to convert it into a probability

$$Probabaility = \frac{1}{1 + e^{-score}}$$

To understand this process, we will break this down using Python. Scoring up our data frame in Python

Program 10-2: Producing logistic model scores

```
# this produces our score, not probability
logistic1['score'] = result.fittedvalues
```

Figure 10.3: Scored logistic output

tier_1	tier_2	tier_3	tier_4	score
0	0	1	0	-1.56713
0	0	1	0	-0.884844
1	0	0	0	1.03771
0	0	0	1	-1.52733
0	0	0	1	-2.00811
0	1	0	0	-0.532346
1	0	0	0	-0.325869
0	1	0	0	-1.28322
0	0	1	0	-1.38171
0	1	0	0	0.0715033

The score is useful to demonstrate how we calculate the probabilities. From figure 10.2, we have our coefficients, but we need more accuracy to produce the score.

Program 10-3: Improved coefficient accuracy code

```
logit_model.fit().params
```

- income = 0.000226
- mortgage = 0.080404
- tier_2 = -0.675443
- tier_3 = -1.340204
- tier_4 = -1.551464
- const = -3.989979

Using ID 1, Tier=3 as an example:

$$Score = interecpt + (income * 0.000226) + (mortgage * 0.080404) + Tier$$

$$Score = -3.98998 + (3800 * 0.000226) + (36.1 * 0.0804) - 1.3402$$

$$Score = -3.98998 + (0.8588) + (2.90244) - 1.3402$$

$$\mathbf{Score = -1.568}$$

The difference is caused by rounding.

Repeating for ID 3, where tier=1

$$Score = interecpt + (income * 0.000226) + (mortgage * 0.0804) + Tier$$

$$Score = -3.98998 + (8000 * 0.000226) + (40 * 0.0804) + 0$$

$$Score = -3.98998 + (1.808) + (3.216) + 0$$

$$Score = \mathbf{1.03402}$$

Again, the difference is caused by rounding, which is of no concern.

However, as mentioned previously, we want the probabilities, not the scores, so we can either calculate it ourselves or get Python to do it. Obviously, we will get Python to do it.

Program 10-4: Producing logistic model probability

```
# this produces our probability
logistic1['pred_y'] = 1 / (1 + np.exp(-logistic1.score))
```

Program 10-4 converts the score into the probability.

$$Probabaility = \frac{1}{1 + e^{-score}}$$

If you choose to get the probabilities straight away, then we could use

Program 10-5: Producing logistic model probability- version2

```
# this produces our probability
logistic1['pred_y1']= result.predict(x)
```

- **logistic1['pred_y1']=**
    - this tells Python that we want to create a new variable in the data frame scored called pred_y1
- **result.predict(x)**
    - This tells Python to use **result** as created earlier
    - **predict(x)**, use the data frame x, and apply the model on it to get our **prediction**

Figure 10.4: Probabilities on the scored logistic output

Index	tier_1	tier_2	tier_3	tier_4	score	pred_y	pred_y1
0	0	1	0	0	-1.56713	0.172627	0.172627
1	0	1	0	0	-0.884844	0.292175	0.292175
2	0	0	0	0	1.03771	0.738408	0.738408
3	0	0	1	0	-1.52733	0.178385	0.178385
4	0	0	1	0	-2.00811	0.118354	0.118354
5	1	0	0	0	-0.532346	0.36997	0.36997
6	0	0	0	0	-0.325869	0.419246	0.419246
7	1	0	0	0	-1.28322	0.217003	0.217003
8	0	1	0	0	-1.38171	0.200735	0.200735
9	1	0	0	0	0.0715033	0.517868	0.517868

As you can see, the probabilities from using the equation, to using Python straight away provides the same answer.

Using our previous example of ID 1 and 3.

$$Probability = \frac{1}{1 + e^{-score}}$$

For ID 1 score = -1.56712

$$Probability = \frac{1}{1 + e^{1.56712}}$$

The negative has disappeared as both negatives cancel each other out.

$$Probability = 0.17262$$

Therefore, the probability of those consumers that match the same criteria of ID 2 of a sale is 17.26%.

For ID 3

$$Probability = \frac{1}{1 + e^{-1.0377}}$$

$$Probability = 0.7384$$

Therefore, the probability of those consumers that match the same criteria of ID 3 of a sale is 73.84%. A common question asked at this stage is 'Why are we calculating the probabilities of events when we have the answers in front of us?' It is so we can apply this model on a different population, so we can maximise our efforts on success e.g. why focus our efforts on a customer with a probability of a sale of 17% when we have another one with 73%? We use statistical models to help us make informed and intelligent choices.

Which should always prompt the next question… 'How do we know if this model is any good?' For a multi-linear regression model, we used adjusted R-squared, but since the logistic curve is not a straight line, we would need something else.

10.3 Logistic measurements

As detailed previously, r-square is not a good measurement for the accuracy of a logistic model. In this book we will use Gini (Somers' D).

- Gini (Somers' D)
    - Although the equations for Gini and Somers D are different, they both have the same answer

10.4.1 Gini (Somers' D)

Before we start providing the code for Gini (Somers' D) we will introduce a couple more concepts ROC (Receiver Operating Characteristic) and AUC (Area Under the Curve).

When we try and predict a binary outcome (e.g. yes/no, sold/not sold), we would consider its true positive rate (TPR) and false positive rate (FPR).

Next follows a very simplistic approach of a mock dataset

Table 10.1: TPR and FPR

Target	Probability	Cumulative target	Cumulative non-target	TPR	FPR
1	0.95	1	0	0.2	0
1	0.85	2	0	0.4	0
0	0.75	2	1	0.4	0.2
1	0.65	3	1	0.6	0.2
0	0.55	3	2	0.6	0.4
1	0.45	4	2	0.8	0.4
0	0.35	4	3	0.8	0.6
1	0.25	5	3	1	0.6
0	0.15	5	4	1	0.8
0	0.5	5	5	1	1

From the above table, we can see how we can calculate the TPR and FPR

- Sort the data by the probability descending
- Cumulatively add the targets
- Cumulatively add the non-targets
- TPR is the cumulative target divided by total targets
- FPR is the cumulative non-target divided by total non-targets

The more targets in the higher end of the probability range, and the more non-targets in the lower end of the probability range, the stronger the model.

Using this data, we can construct our ROC chart.

Table 10.2: TPR and FPR data for the graph in Excel

Target	Probability	Cumulative target	Cumulative non-target	TPR	FPR	base
				0	0	0
1	0.95	1	0	0.2	0	0.1
1	0.85	2	0	0.4	0	0.2
0	0.75	2	1	0.4	0.2	0.3
1	0.65	3	1	0.6	0.2	0.4
0	0.55	3	2	0.6	0.4	0.5
1	0.45	4	2	0.8	0.4	0.6
0	0.35	4	3	0.8	0.6	0.7
0	0.25	5	3	1	0.6	0.8
1	0.15	5	4	1	0.8	0.9
0	0.5	5	5	1	1	1

Put this data into Excel, then construct a scatter plot on the TPR, FPR columns together.

Figure 10.5: TPR and FPR data in Excel

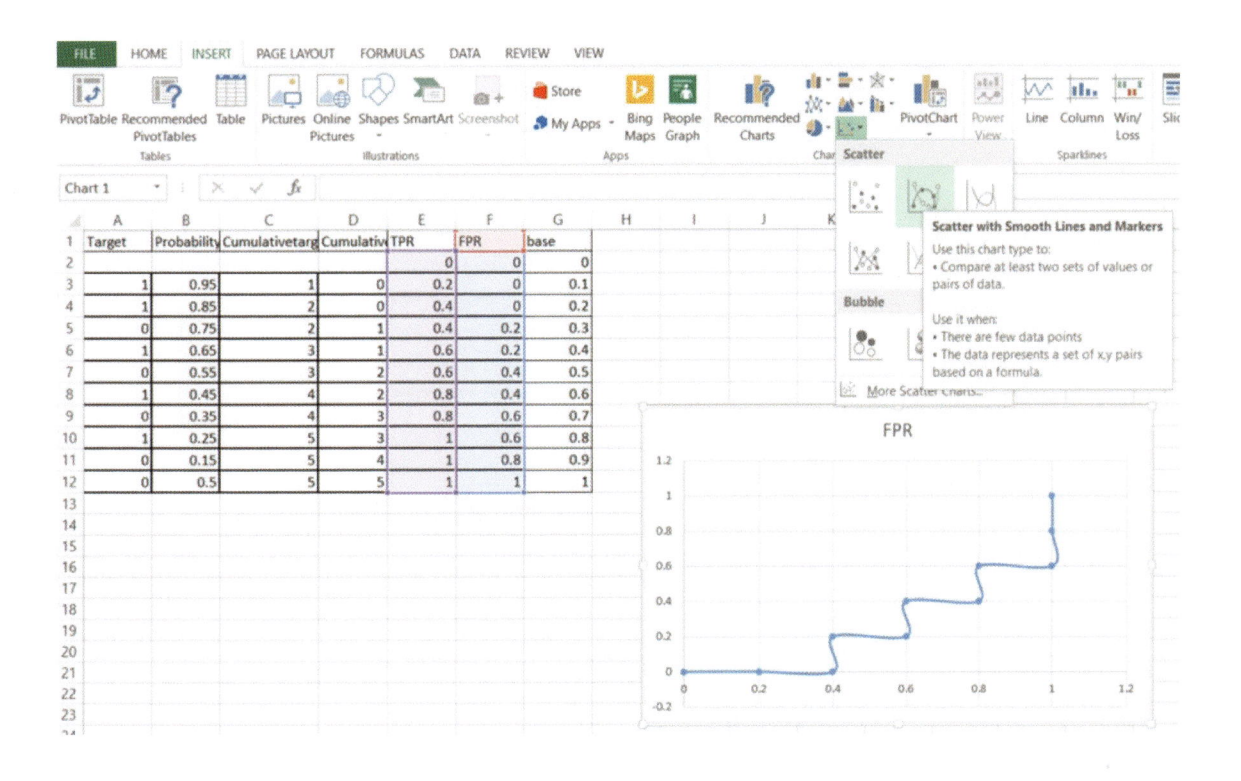

Just as we did in chapter 1.4.

Next add a base to the graph, with the base being both the X and Y axis.

Figure 10.6: Plotting TPR and FPR data in Excel

The reason why we included the zeroes, is to construct the graph so everything starts at 0, 0 on the graph.

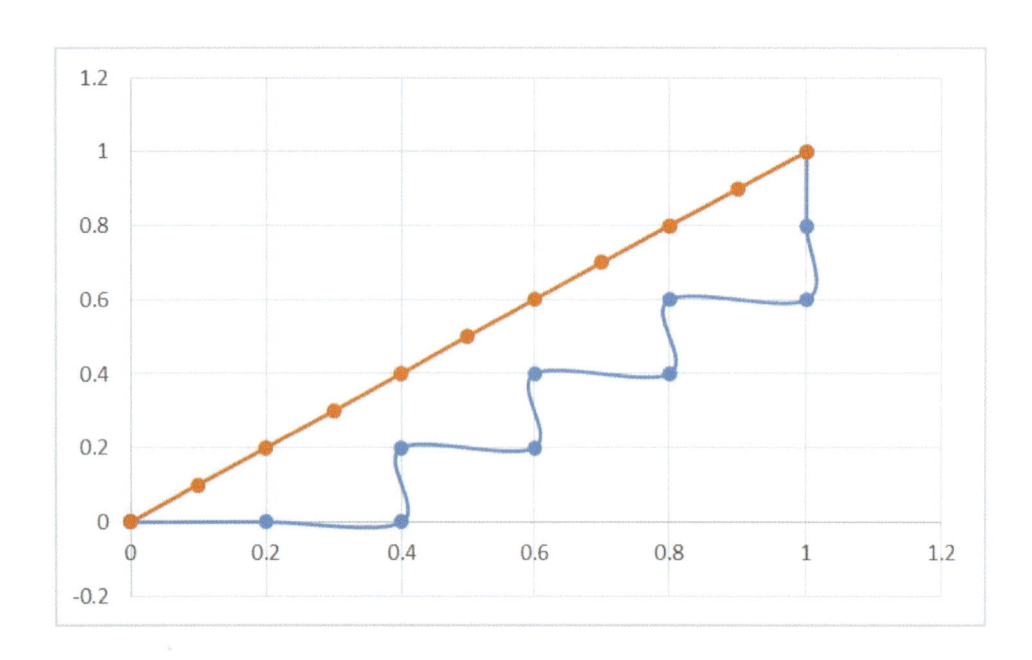

Figure 10.7: Chart of TPR and FPR data

This is an example of a ROC chart. The ROC is used to evaluate the performance of a logistic model. In this example, the TPR is on the x-axis. It is a rare occurrence to build a ROC chart with such few observations (rows), as we get a wobbly curve.

If the plot followed the straight line from the lower left to the upper right (baseline), then the model cannot differentiate between the target and non-target, so it has no power. From the graph, we can see that there is space between the base (AUC) and the curve, so there is power in this model

The performance is then calculated by calculating the Area Under the Curve (AUC). This gives you a score between 0 and 1. A score of 0.5 means that there is no power, with any values closer to one being more predictive, which will lead us to calculate the Gini (or Somers' D)

$$Gini = (2 * AUC) - 1$$

Gini tells us how well the model separates the targets and non-targets using the probability. Python can able us to calculate Gini by using it to compute the Area under the curve (AUC).

First of all, save the table as a CSV file, (in this example it's called roc.csv).

Table 10.3: Roc.csv

Target	Probability	Cumultarget	Cumulnontarget	TPR	FPR
1	0.95	1	0	0.2	0
1	0.85	2	0	0.4	0
0	0.75	2	1	0.4	0.2
1	0.65	3	1	0.6	0.2
0	0.55	3	2	0.6	0.4
1	0.45	4	2	0.8	0.4
0	0.35	4	3	0.8	0.6
0	0.25	5	3	1	0.6
1	0.15	5	4	1	0.8
0	0.5	5	5	1	1

Program 10-6: Calculating AUC and Gini in Python

```
# import data
roc = pd.read_csv("C:/temp/roc.csv")


#activate
from sklearn.metrics import roc_auc_score


# run function
AUC = roc_auc_score(roc.Target, roc.Probability)
#calculate gini
```

1. AUC = roc_auc_score(roc.Target, roc.Probability)
    a. **AUC** is our output file
    b. **roc_auc_score** tells Python the function we want to use
    c. **roc.Target, roc.Probability**, this tells Python the field with the probability and what we are trying to predict
2. Gini = (2 * AUC) -1
    a. Our Gini calculation
3. AUC= 0.68
4. Gini =0.36

At this stage, people tend to ask, "what is a good Gini?" Alas, there is no definite answer, as it depends on data quality, the industry you are in and does the new model out-perform the previous model. If you create a new model and it does not out-perform the old one, then questions will be raised about why they should use the new model.

10.4 Performance of initial logistic model

Using the data frame logistic1, created in program 10.4, our first step will be creating a ROC curve using Python.

Program 10-7: ROC in Python

```
from sklearn.metrics import roc_curve
import matplotlib.pyplot as plt

#get our fpr and tpr
fpr, tpr, thresholds = roc_curve(logistic1.sold, logistic1.pred_y)


plt.plot(fpr, tpr, 'orange')


#plots a straight line - our base
plt.plot([0, 1], [0, 1],'black')


#labels
plt.xlabel('False Positive Rate')
plt.ylabel('True Positive Rate')
plt.title('Receiver operating characteristic')
plt.show()
```

As always we follow the same pattern, active library, run function to gather our statistics/graph. In this instance, the function **roc_curve**, provides us with our key statistics **tpr** and **fpr (thresholds** is not covered in this book). The plot commands have been covered in chapter 4.

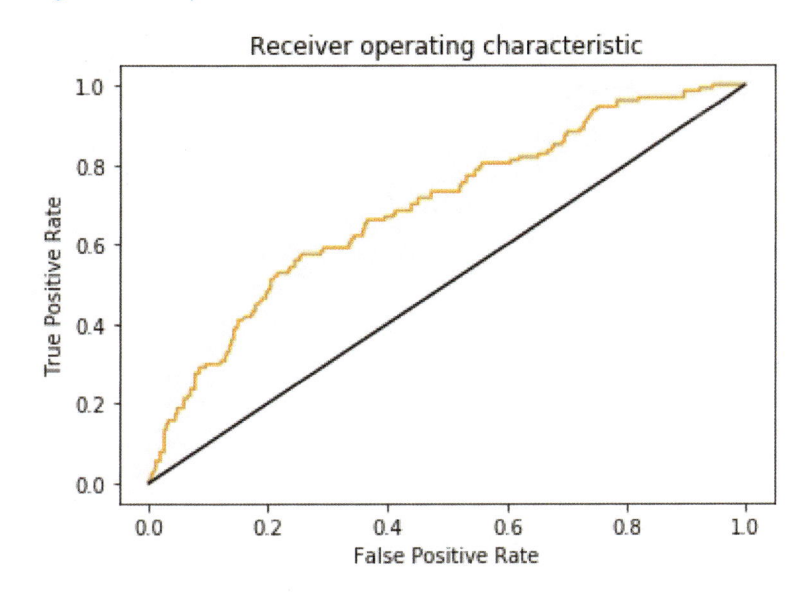

Figure 10.8: Python ROC

Next part entails calculating our AUC and Gini. We have already covered this therefore; the code is as follows.

Program 10-8: Calculating AUC and Gini

```
AUC = roc_auc_score(logistic1.sold, logistic1.pred_y)
Gini = (2 * AUC) -1


AUC
Gini
```

AUC=0.6928

Gini = 0.3856

10.5 Creating a scorecard

10.5.1 Exercise 10.1: logistic model

This exercise will use a combination of previously covered material to generate a scorecard. Your company wants to market a high-end product to its customers. Their key strategy is that they do not want to market to customers that will go bankrupt in the future. Import the data sample.csv (in chapter 5) and replace the missing values CCJ_government and CCJ_private with a 0.

Use this data to create a logistic scorecard predicting the likelihood of a customer going bankrupt (target=1), using the variables:
- CCJ_government
- CCJ_private
- bank_balance
- properties
- amount_owed

Write up the scorecard to produce a probability. Check if your calculations match the Python solution. Measure the performance of this model producing:
- ROC chart
- AUC value
- Gini value

10.5.1 Solution to exercise 10.1

Program 10-9: Exercise 9.1 Solution part 1

```python
#exercise9.1

import numpy as np
import pandas as pd

#import data
sample = pd.read_csv("C:/temp/sample.csv")

#update nulls
sample['CCJ_government'] = sample['CCJ_government'].fillna(0)
sample['CCJ_private'] = sample['CCJ_private'].fillna(0)


#create our target
y = sample['target']

# our predictor variables
x = sample[['CCJ_government', 'CCJ_private', 'bank_balance', 'properties', 'amount_owed'  ]]

# add constant
x['const'] = 1

# call our library
import statsmodels.api as sm

#the model code
logit_model=sm.Logit(y,x)

#the results
result=logit_model.fit()
print(result.summary())

# put on score and probabilities

sample['score'] = result.fittedvalues
sample['pred']= result.predict(x)
```

Program 10-10: Exercise 9.1 Solution part 2

```
#measurements and plots
from sklearn.metrics import roc_auc_score
from sklearn.metrics import roc_curve
import matplotlib.pyplot as plt

#get out fpr and tpr
fpr, tpr, thresholds = roc_curve(sample.target, sample.pred)

#chart code
plt.plot(fpr, tpr, 'orange')
#plots a straight line - our base
plt.plot([0, 1], [0, 1],'black')
#labels
plt.xlabel('False Positive Rate')
plt.ylabel('True Positive Rate')
plt.title('Receiver operating characteristic')
plt.show()

#measurements
AUC = roc_auc_score(sample.target, sample.pred)
Gini = (2 * AUC) -1

AUC
Gini
```

The solution has been broken down into 6 segments

1) Importing and basic data cleansing

```
#import data
sample = pd.read_csv("C:/temp/sample.csv")

#update nulls
sample['CCJ_government'] = sample['CCJ_government'].fillna(0)
sample['CCJ_private'] = sample['CCJ_private'].fillna(0)
```

Possibly, you referred to the previous chapters for this code. As mentioned previously, if we have the code ready to use… use it.

2) Create our target and predictor variables

```
#create our target
y = sample['target']


# our predictor variables
x = sample[['CCJ_government', 'CCJ_private', 'bank_balance', 'properties', 'amount_owed' ]]
```

The only tip I can provide here is to ensure that you have not added any uppercase letters when typing out the variables.

3) Creating the model with results

```
# call our library
import statsmodels.api as sm


#the model code
logit_model=sm.Logit(y,x)


#the results
result=logit_model.fit()
print(result.summary())
```

Figure 10.9: Logistic result for exercise 10.1

```
                          Logit Regression Results
==============================================================================
ep. Variable:                  target   No. Observations:                13508
odel:                           Logit   Df Residuals:                    13502
ethod:                            MLE   Df Model:                            5
ate:                 Thu, 30 Apr 2020   Pseudo R-squ.:                  0.3315
ime:                         13:39:34   Log-Likelihood:                -2582.7
onverged:                        True   LL-Null:                       -3863.4
ovariance Type:             nonrobust   LLR p-value:                     0.000
==============================================================================
                   coef    std err          z      P>|z|      [0.025      0.975]
------------------------------------------------------------------------------
CJ_government    1.1349      0.055     20.560      0.000       1.027       1.243
CJ_private       0.9864      0.086     11.458      0.000       0.818       1.155
ank_balance     -0.0025      0.000    -12.841      0.000      -0.003      -0.002
roperties       -0.5359      0.088     -6.118      0.000      -0.708      -0.364
mount_owed       0.0004   4.56e-05      9.708      0.000       0.000       0.001
onst            -2.4230      0.049    -49.636      0.000      -2.519      -2.327
==============================================================================
```

From the results, we get our score calculation.

Now we can calculate our score

> **Score** = -2.423 + (*CCJ_government* * 1.135) + (*CCJ_private* * 0.9864) + (*bank_balance* * -0.00254) + (*properties* * -0.539) + (*amount_owed* * 0.0004424)

4) Scoring and calculating the probability

> sample['score'] = result.fittedvalues

Figure 10.10: Attaching scores to the data frame

Index	_owed	ages_debt_percer	stocks_profile	rence_wages_last	properties	mortgage	score
0		100	1.5	-0.2	1	0	-7.73444
1		100	26.2	0	2	1	-89.7324
2		63.6	31.5	0.2	0	0	-45.2665
3		100	-170.2	-0.9	0	0	-2.71356
4		100	12.9	0	10	1	-8.45261
5		100	84.9	0.1	0	0	-4.07681
6		0	-0.9	0	1	0	-7.05152
7		74.6	783.1	0	7	1	-6.39452
8		100	7.9	0	0	0	-5.43374
9		100	11.6	0.2	1	1	-2.95885

Using ID 1 as our example:
- CCJ_government = 0
- CCJ_private = 0
- bank_balance = 1884
- properties = 1
- amount_owed = 24

> **Score** = -2.423 + (*CCJ_government* * 1.135) + (*CCJ_private* * 0.9864) + (*bank_balance* * -0.00254) + (*properties* * -0.539) + (*amount_owed* * 0.0004424)

> **Score** = -2.423 + (*0* * 1.135) + (*0* * 0.9864) + (*1884* * -0.00254) + 1 * -0.539) + (*24* * 0.0004424)

> **Score** = -2.423 + 0 + 0 - 4.78536 - 0.539 + 0.01068
> = **-7.736**

Using ID 2 as our next example:
- CCJ_government = 0
- CCJ_private = 0
- bank_balance = 33946
- properties = 2
- amount_owed = 1

> **Score** = -2.423 + (*0* * 1.135) + (*0* * 0.9864) + (*33946* * -0.00254) + (2 * -0.539) + (1 * 0.0004424)

> **Score** = -2.423 + 0 + 0 - 86.2228 - 1.078 + 0.0000442
> = **-89.7234**

Difference between Python results and ours (as mentioned previously) is due to rounding.

```
sample['pred']= result.predict(x)
```

Figure 10.11: Attaching probabilities to the data frame

rofile	rence_wages_last_	properties	mortgage	score	pred
-0.2	1	0	0	-7.73444	0.000437306
0	2	1	0	-89.7324	1.07076e-39
0.2	0	0	0	-45.2665	2.19291e-20
-0.9	0	0	0	-2.71356	0.062178
0	10	1	0	-8.45261	0.000213297
0.1	0	0	0	-4.07681	0.0166786
0	1	0	0	-7.05152	0.000865346
0	7	1	0	-6.39452	0.0016679
0	0	0	0	-5.43374	0.00434775
0.2	1	1	0	-2.95885	0.04932
0	1	0	0	-2.98414	0.0481476

Calculating the probability is easy, is when we have the score

$$Probability = \frac{1}{1 + e^{-score}}$$

For ID1, the score = -7.734440

$$Probability = \frac{1}{1 + e^{-(-7.7344)}}$$

$$Probability = \frac{1}{1 + e^{7.7344}}$$

$$Probability = 0.000437$$

$$Probability = 0.0437\%$$

So ID1 has 0.0437% chance of going bankrupt.

5) Producing the ROC chart

```
#measurements and plots

from sklearn.metrics import roc_auc_score

from sklearn.metrics import roc_curve

import matplotlib.pyplot as plt


#get out fpr and tpr

fpr, tpr, thresholds = roc_curve(sample.target, sample.pred)


#chart code

plt.plot(fpr, tpr, 'orange')

#plots a straight line - our base

plt.plot([0, 1], [0, 1],'black')

#labels

plt.xlabel('False Positive Rate')

plt.ylabel('True Positive Rate')

plt.title('Receiver operating characteristic')

plt.show()
```

Figure 10.12: ROC chart for exercise 10.1

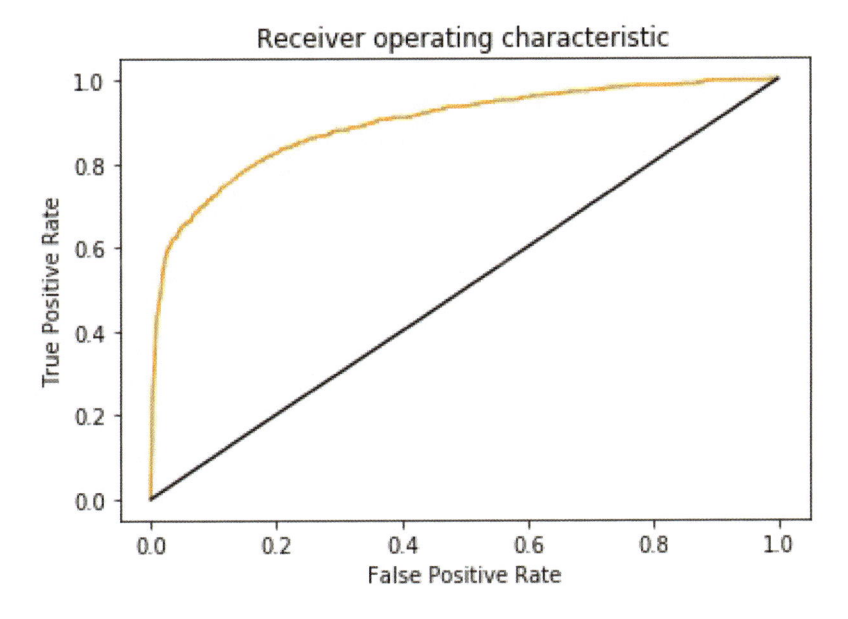

From the graph, we can tell that we are going to have a big AUC figure, which implies that the model will be very predictive.

6) Calculating AUC and Gini

```
#measurements
AUC = roc_auc_score(sample.target, sample.pred)
Gini = (2 * AUC) -1


AUC
Gini
```

With an AUC value of 0.8939 and a Gini of 0.7877, these figures confirm that the model is good at predicting the outcome.

10.6 Summary

This chapter will hopefully understand the basics and key measurements when we build a logistic model.

In a real-life scenario, the model building process would use more variables, require further testing and plenty of issues (usually data).

11 Finale

This book was created to be the book before the book.

Experienced analysts can do extremely clever analysis using powerful computers, but without understanding some of the basics described here, they repeat the same mistakes I have observed in many industries.

As you may have noticed, this book has minimalized the theory aspects, as I have found application more useful in real-life.

Some key simple statistics can be calculated in Excel, which is why, whenever possible, I like using Excel to explain statistics.
You cannot hide your results/findings when it is all to see, which promotes openness and knowledge transfer.

If you like this book, you may be interested in the next book, which details how to build statistical models in the workplace. This new book builds on the foundations covered here to produce a book that can create a statistical modeller.

List of tables

Table 1.1: Exercise 1.1 data 13

Table 1.2: Correlation data 15

Table 1.3: Correlation results 15

Table 1.4: Exercise 1.4 correlation data 22

Table 1.5: Simple linear regression data 24

Table 1.6: Exercise 1.3 data 29

Table 2.1: Example 2.1 data 34

Table 2.2: Exercise 2.1 data 36

Table 2.3: Example for chi-square data 38

Table 2.4: Exercise 2.2 data 39

Table 3.1: Chi-square results 67

Table 3.2: Tier statistics results 68

Table 4.1: Comparing Excel and Python code for correlation 80

Table 4.2: Python Correlation results 80

Table 4.3: Simple linear regression data 83

Table 4.4: Example 2.1 data 86

Table 4.5: Initial results 88

Table 4.6: Data for chi-square analysis 89

Table 5.1: Dataset description 95

Table 5.2: Further expressions 99

Table 5.3: Simple statistics code 101

Table 5.4: Key Python commands summarised 112

Table 6.1: Chapter 6 sample code 122

Table 7.1: Table of Results 126

Table 7.2: Example 7.3 results 129

Table 7.3: Exercise 7.1 results 131

Table 7.4: Chapter 7 sample code 141

Table 8.1: Mean, median, mode and range 144

Table 8.2: Figures for calculating simple linear regression 145

Table 8.3: X*Y and X² 146

Table 8.4: Calculating key figures for r-squared 148

Table 9.1: T-statistic significance rating 159

Table 10.1: TPR and FPR 180

Table 10.2: TPR and FPR data for the graph in Excel 181

Table 10.3: Roc.csv 183

List of figures

Figure 1.1: List of numbers in Excel 9

Figure 1.2: Average command in Excel 10

Figure 1.3: Average command in Excel 11

Figure 1.4: Results of average, median and mode in Excel 11

Figure 1.5: Range, variance, standard deviation and standard error in Excel 12

Figure 1.6: Exercise1.1 solution 14

Figure 1.7: Renaming an Excel sheet 16

Figure 1.8: Creating a scatter graph 17

Figure 1.8: Adding further plots in a scatter graph (1) 18

Figure 1.9: Adding further plots in a scatter graph (2) 18

Figure 1.10: Adding further plots in a scatter graph (3) 19

Figure 1.11: Correlation graphs 20

Figure 1.12: Changing the appearance of a graph (1) 21

Figure 1.13: Changing the appearance of a graph (2) 21

Figure 1.14: Correlation plot 22

Figure 1.15: Correlation solution 23

Figure 1.16: Scatter plot for simple linear regression.. 25

Figure 1.17: Adding a trendline... 25

Figure 1.18: Selecting equation and r-square 26

Figure 1.19: Simple linear regression graph 27

Figure 1.20: R-square plots 28

Figure 1.21: Linear chart for exercise 1.3 30

Figure 2.1: Normal distribution plot 31

Figure 2.2: Positive skewed distribution   Figure 2.3: Negative skewed distribution 32

Figure 2.4: Two-tailed verses one-tailed hypothesis 33

Figure 2.5: T-Test results.. 35

Figure 2.6: Exercise 2.1 t-test results.. 37

Figure 2.7: Expected results for chi-square 38

Figure 2.8: Chi-square formula in Excel 39

Figure 2.9: Chi-square solution for exercise 2.2 40

Figure 2.10: Chi-square test of association data.. 41

Figure 2.11: Chi-square test of association results 41

Figure 3.1: Example of a decision tree... 44

Figure 3.2: Creating categorical variables (1) 46

Figure 3.3: Snapshot of the Excel sheet where sold=1 46

Figure 3.4: Creating the new bins using copy and paste 48

Figure 3.5: Example of an 'if' statement in Excel.. 49

Figure 3.6: Click and drag function in Excel (1).. 49

Figure 3.7: Click and drag function in Excel (2).. 50

Figure 3.8: Click and drag function in Excel (3).. 50

Figure 3.9: Click and drag function in Excel – all of the if statements 51

Figure 3.10: Excel formula for income group: 51

Figure 3.11: Excel formula for mortgage group.. 52

Figure 3.12: Excel formula for mortgage group 53

Figure 3.13: Completed Excel sheet 53

Figure 3.14: Creating a new column 55

Figure 3.15: Excel new column completed 55

Figure 3.16: Pivot table creation (1) 56

Figure 3.17: Pivot table creation (2) 56

Figure 3.18: Pivot table creation (3) 57

Figure 3.19: Pivot table selecting rows and values 58

Figure 3.20: Pivot table creating a calculated field (1) 58

Figure 3.21: Pivot table creating a calculated field (2) 59

Figure 3.22: Pivot table creating a calculated field (3) 59

Figure 3.23: Pivot table creating a calculated field (4) 60

Figure 3.24: Formatting a pivot table (1) 60

Figure 3.25: Formatting a pivot table (2) 61

Figure 3.26: Formatting a pivot table (3) 61

Figure 3.27: Formatting a pivot table (4) 62

Figure 3.28: Formatting a pivot table (5) 62

Figure 3.29: Formatting a pivot table (5) 63

Figure 3.30: Formatting a pivot table (6) 63

Figure 3.31: Formatting a pivot table - completed 64

Figure 3.32: Creating expected sales column for chi-square 64

Figure 3.33: Result of expected sales column 65

Figure 3.34: Chi-square result of tier 65

Figure 3.35: Calculating the chi-square for income 66

Figure 3.36: Chi-square for income 66

Figure 3.37: Chi-square for mortgage 67

Figure 3.38: Initial decision tree 68

Figure 3.39: Conditional formatting for decision tree creation 69

Figure 3.40: Final decision tree 69

Figure 4.1: Spyder 72

Figure 4.2: Activating libraries 73

Figure 4.3: Code section 74

Figure 4.4: Variable explorer 74

Figure 4.5: Console section 74

Figure 4.6: First error in Python 75

Figure 4.7: Calculating the mean in Python 76

Figure 4.8: Results from calculating the median 76

Figure 4.9: Results from calculating the range 77

Figure 4.10: Results from calculating further statistics 77

Figure 4.11: Results from figure 1.5 78

Figure 4.12: Copy of figure 1.11 78

Figure 4.13: Python results for correlation 80

Figure 4.14: Initial plot 81

Figure 4.15: Final Correlation plot 82

Figure 4.16: Our model 84

Figure 4.17: Chart of simple linear regression with trendline 86

Figure 4.18: Creating arrays for t-test 87

Figure 4.19: Dataframe chi_data 90

Figure 4.20: initial results 91

Figure 5.1: Variable Explorer pane 96

Figure 5.2: Data frame top 20 96

Figure 5.3: info() 97

Figure 5.4: Using the environment pane 98

Figure 5.5: Using the variable explorer pane 99

Figure 5.6: Basic expressions results 100

Figure 5.7: Results from 'and' and 'or' 101

Figure 5.8: Results using characteristic variables 104

Figure 5.9: Pre-post results of amending null values.. 106

Figure 5.10: Results of adding new columns to sample data frame 108

Figure 5.11: Correcting infinity calculations 109

Figure 5.12: Rounding values in columns 109

Figure 5.13: Results of 'np.where' command 111

Figure 5.14: Solution to exercise 5.2... 112

Figure 6.1: Data frame mockdata 116

Figure 6.2: Diagram of a full join... 118

Figure 6.3: Full join result.. 119

Figure 6.4: Diagram of an exclusive join 120

Figure 6.5: Diagram of exclusive join (2)... 120

Figure 6.6: Diagram of appending join.. 121

Figure 7.1: Results... 126

Figure 7.2: Calculating percentages results 127

Figure 7.3: Full results to example 7.3.1 129

Figure 7.4: View of summar3 134

Figure 7.5: Exporting data into Excel 135

Figure 7.6: Simple MI report 135

Figure 7.7: Exercise 7.2 report in Excel 140

Figure 8.1: Normal distribution... 143

Figure 8.2: Python simple linear regression results.. 149

Figure 8.3: Simple linear regression results 151

Figure 9.1: Multiple linear regression results 156

Figure 9.2: The output file with the predicted result 157

Figure 9.3: Solution to Exercise 9.1... 159

Figure 9.4: T-statistics for drink 160

Figure 9.5: New solution for predicting drinks remaining 161

Figure 9.6: Exercise 9.2 part1 results 163

Figure 9.7: Exercise 9.2 part2 results 163

Figure 9.8: Exercise 9.2 part 3 results 164

Figure 9.9: Exercise 9.2 part 4 results 165

Figure 9.10: Exercise 9.3 part1 169

Figure 9.11: Exercise 9.3 part1 170

Figure 9.12: Exercise 9.3 part1 171

Figure 10.1: Logistic graph plot 172

Figure 10.2: Python logistic output 175

Figure 10.3: Scored logistic output 176

Figure 10.3: Probabilities on the scored logistic output 178

Figure 10.4: TPR and FPR data in Excel 181

Figure 10.5: Plotting TPR and FPR data in Excel 182

Figure 10.6: Chart of TPR and FPR data 182

Figure 10.7: Python ROC 185

Figure 10.8: Logistic result for exercise 10.1 189

Figure 10.9: Attaching scores to the data frame 190

Figure 10.10: Attaching probabilities to the data frame 192

Figure 10.11: ROC chart for exercise 10.1 193

Table of programs

Program 4-1: Initial libraries 72

Program 4-2: Creating a list of numbers 73

Program 4-3: Calculating the mean 75

Program 4-4: Calculating the median 76

Program 4-5: Calculating the range in Python 76

Program 4-6: Calculating further statistics 77

Program 4-7: Creating the correlation data 79

Program 4-8: Calculating the correlation in Python 79

Program 4-9: import the plotting library 81

Program 4-10: Plot one line 81

Program 4-11: Plot all lines 82

Program 4-12: Create our arrays 83

Program 4-13: Our simple linear regression code 84

Program 4-14: Plotting simple linear regression model code 85

Program 4-15: Initial statistic analysis 88

Program 4-16: T-test statistic 88

Program 4-17: Chi-square, part 1 create our arrays 90

Program 4-18: Chi-square, part 2 convert arrays to data frame 90

Program 4-19: Chi-square, part 3 chi-square test 91

Program 4-20: Chi-square, part 4 chi-square test 91

Program 4-21: Chi-square, part 5 chi-square p-value 91

Program 5-1: Importing CSV file 94

Program 5-2: viewing top 20 rows of sample 95

Program 5-3: Sample metadata 96

Program 5-4: Equal to 98

Program 5-5: Other expressions 100

Program 5-6: AND command 101

Program 5-7: OR command 101

Program 5-8: Solution to exercise 5.1 102

Program 5-9: Character data frame 103

Program 5-10: Character variable data manipulation 103

Program 5-11: Updating null values 105

Program 5-12: Creating a new column 106

Program 5-13: Creating a date column 107

Program 5-14: Creating a new column based on other columns 107

Program 5-15: Creating a new column based on other columns-2 107

Program 5-16: Using np.where command 108

Program 5-17: Rounding numbers 109

Program 5-18: Creating a categorical column based on another column 110

Program 5-19: Solutionto exercise 5.2 111

Program 6-1: Importing data 114

Program 6-2: Creating two new variables 115

Program 6-3: Creating a new variable with where 115

Program 6-4: Creating the mock_date column 116

Program 6-5: Selecting the columns 116

Program 6-5: Random selection of rows 117

Program 6-6: Creating mocksamp 117

Program 6-7: Full/ Outer join 118

Program 6-8: Right join 120

Program 6.9: Code for inner join 121

Program 6.10: Code for Concatenating join 121

Program 7-1: Creating our data frame 124

Program 7-2: Simple statistics using a data frame 124

Program 7-3: Creating a new data frame and variable 125

Program 7-4: Creating a new data frame and variable 125

Program 7-5: solution to example 7.3.1 127

Program 7-6: Full solution to example 7.3.1 128

Program 7-7: Full solution to exercise 7-1 130

Program 7-8: Summarising and averaging 132

Program 7-9: Exercise 7.4.1 133

Program 7-10: Exporting data to a csv file for Excel 134

Program 7-11: Exercise 7.2 138

Program 8-1: Simple linear regression 148

Program 8-2: Simple linear regression – Exercise 150

Program 9-1: Example 9-1 Multi linear regression 155

Program 9-2: Obtaining predicted value 157

Program 9-3: Exercise 9.1 Multi linear regression 158

Program 9-4: Exercise 9.1 Multi linear regression without X1 160

Program 9-5: Exercise 9.2 part1 162

Program 9-6: Exercise 9.2 part2 163

Program 9-7: Exercise 9.2 part3 164

Program 9-8: Exercise 9.2 part4 165

Program 9-9: Exercise 9.3 part1 168

Program 9-10: Exercise 9.3 part2 169

Program 9-11: Exercise 9.3 part3 170

Program 10-1: First logistic model 174

Program 10-2: Producing logistic model scores 175

Program 10-3: Improved coefficient acuracy code 176

Program 10-4: Producing logistic model probability 177

Program 10-5: Producing logistic model probability- version2 177

Program 10-6: Calculating AUC and Gini in Python 184

Program 10-7: ROC in Python 185

Program 10-8: Calculating AUC and Gini 186

Program 10-9: Exercide 9.1 Solution part 1 187

Program 10-10: Exercise 9.1 Solution part 2 188

Printed in Great Britain
by Amazon